From

The God In Real Time Life Series

The Golden Rule of Love:

The Measure of Everything

By

Dennis R. Madden MA LPC

February 2016

The God In Real Time Life Series

1. **God in Real Time:** The Theology of Empowering Change

2. **Living the Authentic Life:** Moving from Conflict to Freedom

3. **The 12 Voices of God:** God Speaks to You, Recognize His Voice, While Discovering Your Own

4. **The God Partnership:** A Spiritual Awakening

5. **Your Marriage as God Imagined...**

6. **The Golden Rule of Love:** The Measurement of Everything

Dedication

I dedicate this book to my wife Linda Jo and our two daughters Amanda Joanne Pitt and Alissa Joy Ward.

Something happened the day that Amanda was born that changed my DNA forever. I finally understood the Love of God that I had so desperately grasped at for so long. I got it. Then Alissa was born and I was covered with joy. I began to understand God's great love more and more.

Through the years of marriage, I have begun to understand the depths of the Father's love and something new, Jesus' great love for us as well.

Now I have granddaughters; Emmaline, Abbigail, and Autumn. For me it has been a real slow process and love has simmered, steamed, boiled, and even overflowed at times. The awesome love of God is surrounding us at all times. We've only to wade into it and begin to embrace it. I am only just beginning to more fully comprehend it.

*"If I speak in the tongues of men or of angels,
but do not have love,
I am only a resounding gong
or a clanging cymbal.
If I have the gift of prophecy
and can fathom all mysteries
and all knowledge,
and if I have a faith that can move mountains,
but do not have love,
I am nothing.
If I give all I possess to the poor
and give over my body to hardship
that I may boast,
but do not have love,
I gain nothing."
1Corinthians 13:1-3*

If I am as spiritual as angels, if I have immeasurable faith to preform incredible miracles, if I possess wisdom beyond Solomon and equal to no one, and even flow in all things prophetically, if I am a great philanthropist and give more than anyone in history, yet do not contain love within my soul, my mind, my heart, and my spirit,

Then I am empty, I gain nothing, and I am nothing!!

So then Love becomes the measure of Everything!

(Author's Paraphrase)

THE GOLDEN RULE:

So in everything,

Do to others what you

would have them do to you,

for this sums up

the Law and the Prophets.

Matt 7:12

Unless otherwise noted, all Bible texts are from THE HOLY BIBLE: NEW INTERNATIONAL VERSION®. NIV®. Copyright © 1973, 1978

Scripture passages marked (*NIV* electronic ed.) are from The Holy Bible: New International Version electronic ed. Grand Rapids: Zondervan, 1996, c1984

Scripture passages marked (ASV) are from the American Standard Version. Oak Harbor, WA: Logos Research Systems, Inc., 1995

Scripture passages marked (NAS) are taken from the NEW AMERICAN STANDARD BIBLE®, Copyright © 1960,1962,1963,1968,1971,1972,1973,1975,1977,1995 by The Lockman Foundation. Used by permission.

Scripture passages marked (NIRV) are taken from the Holy Bible, New International Reader's Version. 1st ed. All rights reserved throughout the world. Used by permission of Zondervan, 1998

Scripture passages marked (KJV) are taken from the King James Version, now in public domain.

In accordance with the U.S. Copyright Act of 1976, the scanning, uploading, and electronic sharing of any part of this book without the permission of the publisher constitute unlawful piracy and theft of the author's intellectual property. If you would like to use material from the book (other than for review purposes), prior written permission must be obtained by contacting the publisher at www.godnrt.org .

Thank you for your support of the author's rights.

"The Golden Rule of Love: The Measure of Everything"
By Dennis R. Madden MA LPC

ISBN-13: **978-1512180527**
ISBN-10: **1512180521**

Copyright 2016, God in Real Time LLC, Argyle, TX Dennis R. Madden All rights reserved.

ACKNOWLEDGEMENTS:

I wish to thank my editorial staff on this project. To **Robert Elm,** who has been the spearhead administrator and chief editor on the entire God in Real Time series starting with our first book, "*Your Marriage as God Imagined*". I give a special thank you to **Karen Crook,** employment specialist and life coach in northern California. Your quick responses and expert work has helped to put a fine quality to this project. I owe you my many thanks. The fact that many have told us it reads well is due to your selfless efforts.

Table of Contents

Introduction: The Heart of Love 11

Understanding Love 19

Real Love: Never Be Fooled Again. 23

Christian Love: Distinctly Different from All Other Faiths 31

Love is a God Thing. 37

Choosing Love: The Power is Within You 43

What's Love Got to Do with It? Health, Happiness, Long Life. 51

Imagine a Culture Without Love 65

The Unraveling of Love 77

Getting Free to Love 83

Love and the Partnership Principle 103

The Rational Case for Love... 121

Love, the Fingerprint of the Divine 127

REFERENCES: 132

Introduction: The Heart of Love

What is love? Some say that it is impossible to define. Others say it is an illusion, a story we tell ourselves that only exists in one's imagination. Others say that it is at the very core of what it means to be a human being.

Then there are those who say God is Love and to know Him is to find and experience love in its purest form. In this book we will explore the impossible, the myth, the humanity, and the divinity of Love. We will hopefully come away with the possibility of understanding your life within the context of love; what it is to know love, to give love, and to experience love. We will look at what it means to eventually become a loving person that leaves a legacy and a footprint of love in the wake of your life here on planet earth for generations to come.

WHAT IS THE 'HEART OF LOVE?'...

This is a question I have posed to thousands of my patients both in the hospital and in my office. I get a rather consistent answer even though my patients are as different as people can possibly be and from every walk of life. What people tell me of the heart of love is to give and receive freely with unconditional demands of anything in return. Yet at the same time there is a very real expectation of return. They describe mutual attraction, appreciation, natural affection, and an affinity towards each-other. They all describe it as a two-way street of give and take, even though over 50% would describe their personal experience as most often giving and not receiving.

The heart of love as I see it is twofold. First it is this giving to another person without reserve and one does so for the joy of caring for another individual. Secondly it does have an expectation of something in return, though not demanded, it is nonetheless expected.

Let's say I do an act of altruism. I give a MacDonald's dinner to the homeless person on the corner. While entering the restaurant I see them there and I get an extra meal and take it to them while leaving. Of course I have no expectation that this person will do anything in return to me or for me. What is my expectation of return in this situation? My expectation of return comes out in a number of ways. First I expect an attitude of gratitude. If I get cussed out while walking away for not getting them a sprite and a coke instead I will not take that very well. Second most everyone will also expect "Karma" to come around for us.

A fellow I have been friends with for some time was recently complaining to me about his unemployment situation. He began to recite all the good things he has been doing for so long. He began telling me that he even gave a car away. Now life was being unfair, "where is God in all this?"

Actually that is a fair question. It tests the motivations of our soul and heart while in the doing of a thing. So obviously where is God in this man's situation? Obviously God has not moved. He is still there and He is still doing this man all kinds of good. His children are all still there, all family members are healthy, and there are still many, many blessings in his life. We have to remember that rain comes and so does drought.

So what is the twist in the story? Expectation! We form expectations and superimpose those over the top of relationships. The trouble is those expectations are all internal to us specifically and tend to have no basis in the real world. In this case my expectation of God may be misplaced and totally based in a false belief system that is in need of being reworked.

Relationships suffer the very same way. It is unavoidable. When you get two people together, there will be a difference of opinion, a difference of right and wrong, of love and neglect, and a difference between pleasure and gratification or abuse. A great book that gives a simple view of this is the Five Love Languages. In that book Dr. Chapman points to the difference of expectation between two people. He makes a powerful observation that in order to speak another person's love language we have to hear that from the other person. In other words, if you wish to make me happy and feel valued by you, then you will have to ask me what makes me happy and what makes me feel valued.

I grew up helping my mom keep the house. I was the youngest of four boys. My brothers used to tease me saying that I would make a good housewife someday. Doing this for my mother brought me great pleasure and reward, just seeing how much it helped her since she worked full time on top of all that she did for us. When I got married I naturally assumed that my wife would and should greatly appreciate my great efforts to help her in all her housework as well. It was not till we were in a discussion group on "The Five Love Languages" that the truth actually came out.

> **The expression of love can be very simple. It can come in a simple act of kindness. But it also is a two way street. It has to be received as kindness as well in order to be complete.**

It turns out that my wife's mother had always put her down for her housework growing up. She was very impatient with her and made her feel bad by redoing everything my wife did. So when I came along with my chipper helpful attitude, she saw this as an act of disapproval. All those years of trying to help her were being tallied up as a huge negative. I had never asked her how it made her feel. I did tell her <u>how it should make her feel</u>, which turned into another negative.

The expression of love can be very simple. It can come in a simple act of kindness. But it also is a two way street. It has to be received as kindness as well in order to be complete. So we are back to where we began with expectation. The same act given to my mother, was received as love, given to my wife was received as a negative. This was not due to my delivery, but rather was due to the expectation of the receiver.

The Bible is full of these types of events. The parable of the talents is one example, Matthew 25:14-30. To one he gave 5 talents, to another he gave 2 and another he gave 1 talent. Then the master went away. Now a talent was about a year's wages. In today's value that might be anywhere for $20,000 to $200,000. Of course the story goes that the one with 5 and the one with 2 both doubled their gifts through investing. They got excited. What if someone gave you $80,000 to $800,000 to invest? You might get excited too. What an opportunity. But not so for the fellow with 1 talent. He took it as an insult. He was angry and accused the master of being unfair, harsh, uncaring, and even of being evil in taking from others what he should not and basically stealing from others. **"You reap, where you have not sown,"** In the end his own perspective was his own reward. He in essence created his own hell.

Think of it for a moment. The same blessing was given to the three, only in different measures. Yet this man brings his own evil expectation to the equation and ultimately misses out on everything. I have seen it happen thousands of times, and have been guilty of the same in my own life.

I have worked with many people who were receiving acts of kindness all the time, yet were maintaining a constant negative interpretation of the actions and attitudes of others around them. So to them, nothing good was happening. Often these people have negative self-esteem, codependency issues, and passive aggressive personality issues. The more entrenched one gets in this belief system the more difficult it is to identify anything that makes them happy. If they cannot identify what makes them happy then others will never be able to make them happy, and eventually they will give up trying. I have seen so many people in the hospital in this exact situation. They have usually tried to commit suicide and will report extensively on all that is wrong with them, internally identifying thirty or more negative internal emotional struggles. Then they state at the conclusion of my intake form that they are kind, loving, always giving, caring for others to a fault, and just not loved back.

You see something is wrong with that picture. It is describing a one-sided relationship. In all my years of counseling or church ministry I have never heard one person describe a healthy love relationship as one-sided. Yet most Christians live a life thinking of God in this way, as more of a one-sided relationship. You might ask God for things when you are in need; "God please heal my child…Help me with my bills…help me win this promotion…" and the list goes on. Rarely do you wait for an answer from God so He can tell you what to do next in order to see that thing happen in your life. Most people never enter into a dialogue or give-and-take relationship with Father God. Perhaps teachers might be responsible for some of this lopsided confusion in teaching that God does not need or desire a relationship with you.

> **Understanding God's love for us is the foundation to understanding our love of self and our love towards others in the world.**

Understanding God's love for us is the foundation to understanding our love of self and our love towards others in the world. I look to the scriptures in this book to answer those questions of how we define love. We will look at romantic love, love of pleasure, love of children and parental love, love of friends and community and finally love of self. We will take a close look at the current movement of altruism and how it relates to love as defined in the Bible.

It is fair to say that love is the law of relationships. Love is that rule or set of rules that governs how we relate to things, even love for the planet and for life itself. We have many laws regulating those as well. The law of love defines what is fair and just and what is evil, contemptable, and even unnatural.

It's funny how we seem to instinctively know when love is absent and being violated, yet still have such a hard time defining or recognizing it at times. Some behaviors we instantly declare as wrong. Someone is in the news for killing a family in their sleep. That is a no-brainer. We immediately call that evil and have a judgment of some sorts as to what needs to happen, who is to blame, and what should have happened.

However when a friend tells you that you're eating too much of that chocolate cake, well now I am not so sure. Is that love? In this situation you might all-of-the-sudden have mixed feelings about that. You might ask yourself, "Who does she think she is? She's no skinny-mini." So you push it away and start to sulk not knowing what to think, and then you see her go for the cake while you have your head turned. Now you call her a little piglet and you both start to laugh. Now you feel love, where a moment ago you felt ambivalence, some hurt, and confusion.

> **In this book we take a detailed look at healthy verses unhealthy love relationships.**

Where love can be seen in certain obvious actions and situations, there seems to be many more that leave us questioning, "What's really going on here?" As a counselor, we deal with the nuances and subliminal messaging all the time. We see it in the look of an eye, versus the rolling of the eye. We see it in the long steady sigh of someone on the phone, or a shortened, choppy, tearful breathing. We see it in the actions of others that are obvious to us, but to the one in the situation, may not be so clear.

In this book we take a detailed look at healthy verses unhealthy love relationships. We take a look at the fact that our society is based upon certain absolute values of love which are actually easily defined, and how we define them every day in our society. We look at how those values are being redefined in our generation to change the very nature and legal structure of our society, perhaps for the next 100 years.

We redefined morality back in the 60s with a moral decision on abortion, and then followed that with the free love movement. Closely following that was the stance of outlawing prayer in schools. We have since been experiencing a massive slide into cohabitation and the quick dissolution of marriage as we have defined it for nearly 2000 years in our western culture. We have now seen our White House turned into a gay flag as our president and our supreme court defied the will of the people and passed their own laws, overturning the laws of the people in a valid election.

Now it is considered illegal and immoral to speak in support of heterosexual marriage and lifestyle as being a moral absolute or standard. If expressed on a job, a person will be subject to being fired. Some have already been thrown into jail for expressing their views publicly.

> **Love as we have defined it is slipping away in one generation.**

This slide in morality has been forewarned to be the final act before many other of our moral standards will be overturned. Love as we have defined it is slipping away in one generation.

This is why it is so important that we look ultimately at where our long held value of authentic love comes from. We need to understand our basis for any truth or moral absolutes, and especially the value of love.

What is man if we are not defined by love? We are but another beast in the field. We will be supplanted and replaced by all that we fear if we do not conquer our great propensity for selfish, self-centeredness, and restore the rule of Love. We will see how there is both a reasonable and rational appeal to moving in this direction for all mankind as well as the individual.

Understanding Love

This is ultimately the Oldest Question of Mankind; "What is love and why should love matter at all?" Since the very dawn of civilization, cultures have been posing this question in one form or another. Here are some historic definitions of Love.

>**Thomas Aquinas** as *"to will the good of another."* [i]
>
>**Aristotle:** *"Love is composed of a single soul inhabiting two bodies"*
>
>**Plato:** *The Madness of love is the greatest of heaven's blessings.*
>
>*"Every heart sings a song, incomplete, until another heart whispers back. Those who wish to sing always find a song. At the touch of a lover, everyone becomes a poet."*
>
>**Gandhi:** *Love is the strongest force the world possesses… Where there is love, there is life."*
>*"Be the change you wish to see in the world."*
>*"When I despair, I remember that all through history the way of truth and love have always won.*
>*There have been tyrants and murderers, and for a time, they can seem invincible, but in the end, they always fall.*
>*Think of it--always."*
>
>**Tao Te Ching:** *"Being deeply loved by someone gives you strength, while loving someone deeply gives you courage."*
>*"I have just three things to teach: simplicity, patience, compassion. These three are your greatest treasures. Simple in actions and in thoughts, you return to the source of being. Patient with both friends and enemies, you accord with the way things are. Compassionate toward yourself, you reconcile all beings in the world."*
>
>*I prize compassion; therefore I am able to be fearless… But men of the present day abandon compassion, yet aim at valiancy… This is death to them… Now when one is compassionate in battle, he will be victorious. When one is compassionate in defending, his defenses will be strong. When Heaven intends to deliver men, it employs compassion to protect them."*[ii]

> *"If you want to awaken all of humanity, awaken all of yourself. If you want to eliminate the suffering in the world, then eliminate all that is dark and negative in yourself. Truly, the greatest gift you have to give is that of your own self-transformation."*

We could fill a book on thoughts and quotes of philosophers alike that have expressed profound ideas and insights on this very real human expression of love. But what does it matter? Love just happens, right? Well actually it does and it doesn't.

In working with so many people in the church and in the counseling environment during my life, I can assure you that love really gets lost in the woods at times. There will be many times in nearly everyone's life when you will be asking yourself two questions; "Do I really love this person?" and "Does this person really love me?" It can be a friend, a lover, a spouse, a child, a parent, a boss, an employee, or anyone, and we cannot exclude God. The question is, do they have my best interest in mind or are they playing me in some way and deceiving me in order to get what they want? Or even worse, am I doing that to someone else?

> **Greeks define love in four separate categories; Agapeo, Phileo, Eros, Storge.**

How God Defines Love

The New Testament was written in Greek and the Greeks define love in four separate categories; Agapeo, Phileo, Eros, Storge.

Agapeo: Unconditional love; the love of God in the renewed mind in manifestation, sacrificial. Selfless. This is the word translated as love in our English language much of the time. This love is of a divine nature. It is based more on an action and not a feeling. Jesus said, *"Whoever has my commands and obeys them, he is the one who loves me."* (John 14:21a) You are probably familiar with John 3:16, *"For God so loved the world that he gave his one and only Son, that whoever believes in him shall not perish but have eternal life."* Agape also describes the self-giving love between a parent and child.

Phileo: Love between friends, genuine affection and appreciation of another.

Eros: The sense of being in love; romantic love, the word we get erotic or sexual love from. Described by God and seen in the Song of Solomon.

Storge: Love of family; Parent/child, siblings, cousins, etc. In a very close family, agape is felt as well.

Love. You know it when you feel it. You know when there is an icy cold presence in the place where love should be. It sends a chill down your spine. Love is palpable. Love is measurable. We have built a society and culture based around the very idea of love.

In spite of how difficult it can be to experience ongoing loving relationships for a lifetime, we still seek love at every opportunity. We pray for those we care about to experience loving relationships for both the long haul and even in short term relationships.

We even teach like Jesus that we should wish love on those who hate us and do mean things to us. Matthew 5:33-34 *"You have heard that it was said, 'YOU SHALL LOVE YOUR NEIGHBOR and hate your enemy.' "But I say to you, love your enemies and pray for those who persecute you, so that you may be sons of your Father who is in heaven."*

Questions to Consider:

How do you define Love?

What are the top 5 things you look for in a loving relationship?

What is a deal breaker that destroys love for you?

Real Love: Never Be Fooled Again.

Real love can be an intimidating thing. It demands that we be honest and vulnerable with others. For many, this is a threat too close to the heart to allow. They have experienced too much rejection and neglect from those who were entrusted with that loving relationship.

For others it grates on the nerve of a belief that they are not worthy of love in the first place. To believe that they are worthy brings such a flood of pain that it is overwhelming and just not manageable. So they vent anger, push away from real relationships, and hide behind blame. It is a place of lifelong bondage, alone in their bitterness.

Love implies a level of trust. The problem with trust is that it can be thwarted and lost in a moment of revelation of selfish motivations at play. Once trust is lost then love flounders in a sea of suspicion and disbelief.

> **We offer here a quick guide to real love versus false love.**

So finding true love is a lifelong endeavor that demands that one be both trusting like a lamb, and at the same time vigilant and discerning like an eagle.

We offer here a quick guide to real love versus false love. We take a look at what authentic and real love is as well as what it is not. The principles of authentic love are based upon accepted principles not only from the Christian world by way of Scripture, but principles that are standards of behavior widely accepted in the Western world. The values of "do no harm", or of confidentiality, the obligation to protect an individual's rights and autonomy, the obligation to relieve distress and to protect the health of the individual and public—these are accepted standards we, in the mental health care profession, use every day. If violated, there are laws that can be enforced and prosecuted. That is how real and solid these principles are.

The most extensive discussion on the topic of love in scripture is from the Apostle Paul. Paul understood a few things about love from the experience he gained from meeting Jesus on the road to Damascus, and his new life that followed.

If you know your Bible history well, then you know that Paul used to be named Saul and was a fervent and radical persecutor of the followers of Jesus. In the language of our day he would be "jihadist." Remember he chased Christians down, beat them, dismembered them, threw them into prison, separated children from parents, destroyed and confiscated their property and possessions, and even killed them. Yet God took the most unlikely candidate and taught him about His great love. That is how he could turn around and teach us about true love. Because he was forgiven and loved so very much by Jesus. So let's start with the basics we find in Paul's writings.

A Look at Definitions

From a biblical perspective, here is a great chart my lifelong friend and this book's first editor uses in his marriage mentoring ministry. It has a perfect application here. This chart clearly illustrates the very obvious differences between natural or fleshly love and Godly love.

Here we come to understand what Biblical Love is, why it is so powerful, and how to apply it to your mate, your family, your church, and the world around you. The Bible challenges us to Love **one another** (Jn. 13:34 - 35) (Jn. 15:9 - 17), Love **your neighbor** (Rom. 13:10), Love **your enemies** (Matt. 5:44), Love **the Lord your God** (Matt. 22:37 – 38) and Husbands, Love **your wives** (Eph. 5:25 - 32). How? "**as Christ loved the Church**....and **gave Himself up for her**". So this is how Biblical Love is to be lived out in our lives.

Biblical Love 1Cor. 13:4 - 8a (NIV)

LOVE	The Opposite of Love
IS PATIENT	Impatient, Short Tempered, Intolerant
IS KIND	Unkind, Harsh, Cruel
DOES NOT ENVY	Envious, Greedy, Covetous
DOES NOT BOAST	Boastful, Bragging, Self Glorifying
IS NOT PROUD	Proud, Conceited, Arrogant
IS NOT RUDE	Rude, Impolite, Discourteous
IS NOT SELF-SEEKING	Selfish, Greedy, Self-Centered
IS NOT EASILY ANGERED	Easily Angered, Irritated, Exasperated
KEEPS NO RECORD OF WRONGS	Unforgiving, Revengeful, Ungracious
DOES NOT DELIGHT IN EVIL	Negative, Uncomplimentary, Unfair
REJOICES WITH THE TRUTH	Lies, Exaggerates, Distorts
ALWAYS PROTECTS	Ridicules, Puts Down, Sarcastic
ALWAYS TRUSTS	Suspecting, Jealous, Disbelieving
ALWAYS HOPES	Untrusting, Pessimistic, Skeptical
ALWAYS PERSEVERES	Gives Up Easily, Quits, No Convictions
NEVER FAILS	**ALWAYS FAILS**

Note that any one of the attributes in the right-hand column will cause your love relationship to fail. Many marriages have failed because of the eroding effect of unloving behavior over time.

Next is an expanded application on the principles of the love chapter in 1 Corinthians 13. Here I look at the applications I have seen as I have applied them to the fields of ministry, industry, and over 10,000 counseling relationships.

Years ago I was introduced to 4 words that defined worldly love. In all my years of trying to bring clarity to understanding love in the multitude of our relationships I have repeatedly seen these 4 words define accurately the opposite of Godly love (what I call here Authentic Love.)

WORLDLY LOVE = INAUTHENTIC	GODLY LOVE = AUTHENTIC
General Expression	
Use	Serves God first
Manipulation	Acknowledges God's control
Domination	Leads authentically (does not manipulate, dominate and control)
Control	Peaceful, Gentle, Kind
	Gives selflessly
Individual Expression	
Controls via deception	Delights in truth, freedom and autonomy
Seeks to benefit self only	Benefits others and self
Focus is immediate desire and lust	Focuses on long term mutual benefit
Seeks self-gratification first	Weighs self-gratification with what is right and most needed for the good of the relationship
Envies	Appreciates
Ambitious to the point of controlling to get one's way	Desires freedom, values empowerment, assists others in meeting needs while honoring own needs—balances both
Endangers self-concept, self-worth of others in order to feel superior	Humbly honors others by valuing and acknowledging their God given abilities and giftings as well as their obligations to fulfill them in life
Group Expression	
Exclusive	Inclusive
Divisive	Brings people together
Refuses reconciliation, ostracizes	Seeks reconciliation and restoration
Sees weakness in bringing people together	Sees strength in unity
Demands obedience and submission	Celebrates freedom and autonomy
Accuses	Confronts
Passes judgments	Discerns and sets healthy boundaries
Neglects needs and rights	Addresses needs and rights; focuses on what is best for all
Keeps individuals in groups weak and isolated	Celebrates the achievements of individuals
Sees collaborative efforts as subversive	Seeks ways to encourage blessings
Denies private ownership	Honors other's possessions
Allows only sanctioned efforts, all others punished as subversive	Encourages and fosters cooperative efforts

If you're paying attention, then about now you are thinking, "Man I am in need of some changes." I can never read this list without coming under conviction about some area of my own life that I need to correct. When you apply these lists to any relationship, be it personal or business, you will be able to see quickly which spirit you are operating out of; ambition or love.

In looking at those 4 words **use, manipulation, domination**, and **control** we can see a basic motivation of this kind of treatment of others. The motivation is one of self-serving at the expense of others. Perhaps more appropriately said, without regard to the cost or effect on others.

In easy modern day terms, it is like the major car manufacturers putting 20 million cars on the road that they know are going to fail in some way. They calculate the amount of money to fix the problem and weigh that against the paying out the lawsuits for wrongful deaths and injuries resulting from their faulty cars. They decide to not fix the cars. It is not cost effective. In essence they decide to just go ahead and kill or injure a certain number of people to achieve a certain amount of profit. It's just about making money right now.

This of course is not acceptable to society in general, yet in business you hear, "it's not personal, it's just business." It is personal to all those who suffered. What this exposes is the use and manipulation under the guise of making a profit. But profit at the expense of someone's life, freedom, and or health is use and manipulation. It is the opposite of love. Do you really want to trust your life to some company that does not care if you live or die?

What is the opposite of using someone? It is to do things for someone that benefits them even if it costs you. Manipulation is selling you a car that I tell you is perfectly good yet I conceal from you that it might kill you and your family. The opposite of manipulation is honesty and integrity. It is being transparent.

So what is the opposite of domination and control? This involves that New Testament teaching on mutual submission. Jesus taught that if we wish to be great in the kingdom of God, then we would be the servant of all. Recently I have been hearing many Christian leaders referring to themselves as 'Generals.' One such TV personality went so far as to say that he had a command structure and if you wanted to talk with him you had to go through the chain of command. If one wishes to exert control over another person to exert their will over another, this runs opposite to the New Testament teaching of love. Jesus always empowered his disciples to be more, accomplish more than they ever thought possible, and to hear God the Father for themselves. Control over others takes their power away and superimposes ones will over another. Love is longsuffering, while domination, inflicts control in order to suffer as little distraction as possible.

Questions to consider:

Have you ever had someone take your power away from you? What was that like? How did it feel? How did they do that?

Have you ever taken power away from someone else? Can you think of how that made them feel?

Have you ever been used or manipulated by anyone? What was the situation? Describe the feeling it left you with.

Have you ever been manipulated in a relationship?

Have you ever been lied to, cheated, or falsely accused in a relationship? How did this affect your ability to forgive and trust again?

Have you identified any relationships in which you are less than loving?

Name 5 steps you can take to be more loving in your present relationships.

Can you identify the difference between caretaking and caregiving?

Are you the kind of person that does things for others, that they can and should be doing for themselves?

Perhaps you are the kind of person that constantly asks others to do things for you that you should be doing for yourself. Can you think of ways that you might be doing that?

If Love never fails, then how has it succeeded in your life?

How has God's love transformed your thinking about love?

How has God's love transformed your behavior?

How has God's love transformed your love for yourself?

How do you define love now that you have read this chapter?

Is this answer different from the previous chapter? If so how and what caused that change?

Christian Love: Distinctly Different from All Other Faiths

Love is a human experience distinctly different from all species on the planet as far as we have been able to observe and understand to this point. Yet for every culture and every religion, only one has made love the center and focal point of all its values and life, and that is Christianity.

Jesus' teachings were unique and radically different from anything that had appeared on the planet before or since. His teachings on Love set him apart from all others. Drawing on the Old Testament to teach, he provided us with a new understanding of who God is, what He is looking for in us, and what He is willing to do in order to reunite us to Himself.

> **God loved us first.**

PRIMARY TEACHINGS ON THE UNIQUENESS OF LOVE IN THE CHRISTIAN FAITH.

In the following scriptures we can see that God loved us first. He (the Father), sent His only begotten son into the world to lay down his life for us. He initiated a love relationship with us. Indeed, Father God has gone to great lengths to demonstrate His unfailing love to you and to me. Not just in the precious gift of Jesus on the cross to pay that eternal price for all our sin, but He also has created the universe, cosmos, and the world you live in just so that you can know Him and enter a relationship with Him.

Through the scriptures we learn that the greatest thing about Christianity is this interpersonal relationship dynamic called Love. Without that you will not be able to experience a connection with the divine (2 Peter 1:3), nor will you be able to walk in confidence, faith or have full assurance of your position with the Father and eternity. You will further not be able to access the precious promises of God nor be able to overcome the failures of the flesh.

In fact according to 2 Peter 1:3-11, the ultimate expression of the Christian faith is to love.

Peter links love with choice in 2 Peter 1:3-11. He gives a progression of 4 choices that lead to 3 results. For Peter kindness, goodness, and love are things each person bears a personal responsibility to achieve, experience, maintain, and demonstrate outwardly, as well as feel inwardly (regardless of how others are treating you). Peter has a lifetime of experience as the first Apostle-Evangelist-Pastor when he wrote this in 2 Peter 1:3-7. We define this in more detail in the chapters, "*Love is a God Thing*", and "*Love and the Partnership Principle*".

> Kindness, goodness, and love are things each person bears a personal responsibility to achieve.

3: His divine power has given us everything we need for life and godliness

Through our True Knowledge (epignosis) of Him who called us by his own glory and goodness. Through these he has given us his very great and precious promises, so that

Through them you may participate in the divine nature and escape the corruption in the world caused by evil desires.

5 For this very reason, make every effort to ADD to your faith: Virtue /goodness (arête) and to goodness, Knowledge (gnosis) and to knowledge, Self-Control; and to self-control, Perseverance; and to perseverance, Godliness; and to godliness, brotherly Kindness; and to brotherly kindness, Love."

Take some time to meditate on the following scriptures and how they apply to your life and your experience with love.

Romans 5:8 "But God demonstrates his own love for us in this: While we were still sinners, Christ died for us."

John 15:9-17 "As the Father has loved me, so have I loved you. Now remain in my love. If you keep my commands, you will remain in my love, just as I have kept my Father's commands and remain in his love. I have told you this so that my joy may be in you and that your joy may be complete.

My command is this: Love each other as I have loved you. Greater love has no one than this: to lay down one's life for one's friends. You are my friends if you do what I command. I no longer call you servants, because a servant does not know his master's business. Instead, I have called you friends, for everything that I learned from my Father I have made known to you. You did not choose me, but I chose you and appointed you so that you might go and bear fruit—fruit that will last—and so that whatever you ask in my name the Father will give you. This is my command: Love each other."

John 3:13-18 "No one has ever gone into heaven except the one who came from heaven—the Son of Man. Just as Moses lifted up the snake in the wilderness, so the Son of Man must be lifted up, that everyone who believes may have eternal life in him.

For God so loved the world that he gave his one and only Son, that whoever believes in him shall not perish but have eternal life. For God did not send his Son into the world to condemn the world, but to save the world through him. Whoever believes in him is not condemned, but whoever does not believe stands condemned already because they have not believed in the name of God's one and only Son."

Mark 12: 28-34 "One of the teachers of the law came and heard them debating. Noticing that Jesus had given them a good answer, he asked him, "Of all the commandments, which is the most important?"

"The most important one," answered Jesus, "is this: 'Hear, O Israel: The Lord our God, the Lord is one. Love the Lord your God with all your heart and with all your soul and with all your mind and with all your strength.' The second is this: 'Love your neighbor as yourself.' There is no commandment greater than these."

"Well said, teacher," the man replied. "You are right in saying that God is one and there is no other but him. To love him with all your heart, with all your understanding and with all your strength, and to love your

neighbor as yourself is more important than all burnt offerings and sacrifices."

When Jesus saw that he had answered wisely, he said to him, "You are not far from the kingdom of God."

Matthew 5:43-48 *"You have heard that it was said, 'Love your neighbor and hate your enemy.' But I tell you, love your enemies and pray for those who persecute you, that you may be children of your Father in heaven. He causes his sun to rise on the evil and the good, and sends rain on the righteous and the unrighteous. If you love those who love you, what reward will you get? Are not even the tax collectors doing that? And if you greet only your own people, what are you doing more than others? Do not even pagans do that? Be perfect, therefore, as your heavenly Father is perfect."*

John 13:34-35 *"A new command I give you: Love one another. As I have loved you, so you must love one another. By this everyone will know that you are my disciples, if you love one another."*

Romans12:10 *"Be devoted to one another in love. Honor one another above yourselves."*

Romans13: 8 *"Let no debt remain outstanding, except the continuing debt to love one another, for whoever loves others has fulfilled the law."*

Gal 5:14 *"For the entire law is fulfilled in keeping this one command: "Love your neighbor as yourself."*

Matthew 7:12 *"So in everything, do to others what you would have them do to you, for this sums up the Law and the Prophets."*

1 Thessalonians 4:9 *"Now about your love for one another we do not need to write to you, for you yourselves have been taught by God to love each other."*

James 2:8 *"If you really keep the royal law found in Scripture, "Love your neighbor as yourself," you are doing right."*

John 16: 26-27 *"In that day you will ask in my name. I am not saying that I will ask the Father on your behalf. No, the Father himself loves you because you have loved me and have believed that I came from God."*

John 17: 24-26 "Father, I want those you have given me to be with me where I am, and to see my glory, the glory you have given me because you loved me before the creation of the world.

Righteous Father, though the world does not know you, I know you, and they know that you have sent me. I have made you known to them, and will continue to make you known in order that the love you have for me may be in them and that I myself may be in them."

Questions to Consider:

Who have you chosen to love, that disliked you?

How have you expressed love for your brothers and sisters in the church?

How have you expressed love for the lost?

Has anyone complimented you on having loving qualities?

Name at least three ways that others have mentioned to you that you show the love of Christ?

Have you ever loved anyone to Jesus or changed their behavior due to love?

Love is a God Thing.

To really understand love one needs to understand God. As stated in the prior chapter Saul, who became Paul, was a radicalized zealot bent on destroying the church. But let's get real here, that 'church' we are referring to were women, children, and fathers. They were real people that were brutally treated by the Jewish powers that demanded submission or death.

But God is longsuffering, patient, and kind. He is full of grace and forgiveness. Jesus appears to Saul on the road to Damascus and confronts him. "I am Jesus whom you are persecuting." Saul converts and receives forgiveness and salvation. Saul's name is changed to Paul. Paul goes on to write nearly half of the New Testament, including a very helpful definition of real authentic love. Where did Paul get this revelation? He got it from God and his salvation experience. He often describes himself as the chief of sinners as he bore in his conscience feelings of guilt and shame for persecuting the church so brutally. Yet Paul is forgiven much.

> **To really understand love one needs to understand God.**

Jesus asked Peter at the dinner table one evening, (Luke 7:47), *"Who loved God more, someone who had been forgiven of great debt or someone forgiven of little debt?" "Therefore, I tell you, her many sins have been forgiven--as her great love has shown. But whoever has been forgiven little loves little."* Jesus' feet were being washed and he was being anointed with costly oil by a woman of ill repute. Jesus is being maligned as well as the woman as "inappropriate" and if Jesus had any common sense about him he would certainly stop this immediately.

How does Jesus respond? Not in a religious way at all. Instead he pronounces that she has been forgiven, that her faith has saved her and she is free to go in peace.

God is not offended by you. He is not put out by your "inappropriateness." God sees your need for grace and forgiveness, for healing and restoration. As we have seen in the scriptures above, God initiates love in many ways: through creation, through redemption, through salvation, through provision of eternal life, and through the operation of the Holy Spirit.

Love comes from God and is centered in God. We find the true meaning of authentic love by understanding the heart of God and His relentless pursuit of us as His offspring.

> **Love comes from God and is centered in God.**

LOVE IS THE SINGLE GREATEST NEW TESTAMENT TEACHING

Jesus teaches us that love is not just for those who treat us well, but also for those who treat us poorly and we might consider an enemy. Love not only completes our understanding of God, but also of ourselves. Since Christ pronounced on the cross, "Father forgive them for they do not know what they are doing," so too we are to forgive others in our own lives. Forgiveness is given even to those actively working to destroy us.

This is a radical break from traditional thinking of his day and of our day still. We are not commanded to get revenge or to attack back. Rather, in the New Testament way to thinking we are to bless with our mouths and bless in action with our deeds those who are cursing us, abusing us, manipulating us and controlling us. By doing this we fulfill the very will and character of God Himself. *Gal 6:2* ***"Carry each other's burdens, and in this way you will fulfill the law of Christ."***

Love in the New Testament church setting is one of mutual submission. It is not a place where one is attempting to impose ones will over another. Leadership is servanthood and the disciples are constantly reminding each other that they are only servants like anyone else.

Love in the New Testament is considered the highest achievement. In 2 Peter chapter 1 we are given 7 attributes that the believer is solely and completely responsible for manifesting in his or her life. These 7 are given in an order of progressive ability. In other words, one does not get to #7 on the list without experiencing the first 6 to some degree.

> **Love in the New Testament is considered the highest achievement.**

What are these seven things we are responsible for?

- **A choosing** to move toward **virtue.**
- The effort to **learn** what we do not know about God, Jesus, the Holy Spirit, and the Christian walk. You can't do what you do not know.
- **Self-control**—an application of what we have learned, about Jesus as well as from Jesus directly. *Matt 11:28 ("learn from me…")*
- **Perseverance-** - we keep on keeping on in our application, learning, and choosing to follow God.
- **Goodness-** - this is the first thing we experience from doing the first 4 steps.
- **Kindness-** - this is the second thing we experience. Our hearts of stone begin to transform and soften towards others.
- **Love-** - The final thing we are responsible for. We experience the ability to love as a direct result of walking out those 6 steps he gives us. Notice we are responsible for giving love, and for feeling loved from others.

Peter then gives us a perspective of how we can feel assurance and confidence in our walk of faith with God and relationships with others. He tells us we will have these things if we just keep moving forward in this process.

In Peter's way of thinking one cannot achieve assurance of their salvation without the experience of love within themselves.

In the three epistles of John, he explicitly states that you cannot be a child of God if you do not walk in love. For him, such a thing is not possible.

1 John 4:7-12 "Dear friends, let us love one another, for love comes from God. Everyone who loves has been born of God and knows God. Whoever does not love does not know God, because God is love. This is how God showed his love among us: He sent his one and only Son into the world that we might live through him. This is love: not that we loved God, but that he loved us and sent his Son as an atoning sacrifice for our sins. Dear friends, since God so loved us, we also ought to love one another. No one has ever seen God; but if we love one another, God lives in us and his love is made complete in us."

John gives many other stern warnings to those who pretend to love but really do not love. To the Apostles it is clear that love is the single most definitive description of what it means to be a Christian. If it is so, it is thus possible to love in such a way, otherwise Christianity is a farce and is just wishful thinking.

We know of course that our Christian ancestors were no farce. They demonstrated their great love with servant's hearts and they laid their lives down for the gospel and for their fellow brethren in the Lord. They gave a witness to what they experienced and knew was true.

Questions to ask.

Is there anyone in your life in the past that you have loved in such a way? List them here…

Is there anyone in your life in the past that you have failed to love in such a way? List them here…

At present is there anyone that is offering offense to you that you need to love? List them here…

    List 7 ways in which you can take steps to demonstrate love toward them.
        How can you pray for them?
        How can you bless them?
        How can you speak of them?

Choosing Love: The Power is Within You

When I read 2 Peter 1:3-7 (See pg. 32), I come away with some very clear understandings of what my personal choices are and what they are not. My first realization is that if I am not experiencing love for anyone then I have some correcting to do. According to Peter it is my personal responsibility both to give and to experience love. While I realize that God's role in my life is to do for me what I cannot do for myself, I see at the same time that I and only I am responsible for feeling and giving love.

In this scripture Peter states that I must be diligent to make sure I add to my faith and experience those 7 things, the last of which is love. That makes love my personal responsibility. I see this as both the action of giving love as well as the experience of receiving and feeling loved. You should also note already that the New Testament, Jesus, and the apostles all require love as an act of our personal choice and will.

Yet I think it is impossible to talk about love as an action alone without the experience of love. Paul states it like this in 1 Corinthians 13, *"If I speak in the tongues of men or of angels, but do not have love, I am only a resounding gong or a clanging cymbal. If I have the gift of prophecy and can fathom all mysteries and all knowledge, and if I have a faith that can move mountains, but do not have love, I am nothing. If I give all I possess to the poor and give over my body to hardship that I may boast, but do not have love, I gain nothing."*

Here Paul states that without the experience of love behind my 'spiritual' actions, I am as empty as a meaningless clanging cymbal. He further states that even if I have so great of faith that I can move mountains and yet am without the experience of love, then I am nothing. Then if I give all that I have and even sacrifice my life in behalf of the poor and yet do not have the love experience, then I gain nothing.

What is Paul saying? Without the love experience you will be empty, meaningless, and you will not gain anything in this life or the next. In Texas we would say that you're "not worth a hill of beans".

He is not saying that what you have given or achieved is meaningless, he is saying that you as a person are left empty and without any meaning to cling to. You become internally bankrupt.

> Without the love experience you will be empty, meaningless, and you will not gain anything in this life or the next.

When I would come into the intensive psychiatric mental health hospital on Saturday mornings and do my groups, the first thing I would do was to pass out a personal inventory. This allowed every patient to disclose to me on one sheet what was going on internally and externally in their life. Nearly everyone filled this out. I must have collected over 6,000 in my tenure of doing that work every weekend.

I saw a pattern in that sheet. I noticed that about 35% of all patients listing 15 to 35 negative responses as to their internal feelings and mood. They included anger, hate, bitter losses, frustration, depression, detachment, isolation, worry, and many others like that. They shared a particular pattern that was very distinct above any other. In my final question of what do you believe about yourself, about 90% answered something along the lines of this; "I am a loving, giving, kind, patient, person that always does for others and others never do for me. I am unloved and treated badly by those that should love me."

Now if you're a mental health professional, then this is classic codependency. Yet if you are a Christian then the formula for love bears some scrutiny. Something is wrong with that picture, anyone would agree.

For me as a Faith Based counselor meeting Christians from all over the world in the inpatient setting, this was challenging to understand how Christian men and women could show up in the Minirth faith based program with so many showing the same patterns.

Now for me, sitting across from two or three people each week that had come to the end of themselves, many having just attempted suicide only days or hours before, I felt compelled to find out what is going on in this picture. If you are doing all the things to give love and yet you are like Paul's description, empty, without meaning, and not worth a pile of beans, what's going on?

What I found as I worked with several psychiatrists including the late Dr. Frank Minirth, was that these people were performing these actions out of a selfish motivation of codependency. Codependency in its simplest definition (covered more in the chapters on codependency and caretaking) is when I am giving in order to get. It's conditional and if I do not get back what I want or demand, then I will choose to be hurt and offended.

> **Codependency in its simplest definition is when I am giving in order to get. It's conditional and if I do not get back what I want or demand, then I will choose to be hurt and offended.**

My willingness to take offense is in itself a confession of the motivation of my own heart. I accuse others of what I am guilty of within my own heart. Codependency is a bankrupt heart that is in constant need of being reassured and placated.

What Peter makes clear above is that if you believe you are loving yet not ever experiencing love, then you are the one responsible to change your heart. Peter gives you the process of reconnecting all the dots and making sense of it all. Take the seven steps and retrace them. Find out where you are disconnected.

Are you disconnected in making a choice to have your life filled with virtue? This is the Turning stage.

Are you disconnected on a lack of knowledge of knowing what is going on inside of yourself? That is your responsibility to figure out and act upon it to gain the knowledge that you are lacking. This is the Learning stage.

Are you disconnected in the doing of what you know is right and necessary? This is the Burning stage, the application. Perhaps you started to apply things in your life and like many resolutions, you began to slip more and more away from the truth.

The 4th step of disconnect is to stop learning from Father God Himself. You become lax in your prayer life and stop listening to Father God. This is perseverance and the process of keeping on keeping on. Peter says that if you just keep moving forward to some degree, then you will be fruitful and have assurance and confidence.

Believe me, when you lose confidence and assurance it is because you have disconnected from one of these 4 steps. These are also given by Jesus in Matthew 11:28-30 in his discourse on 'coming to find rest.' *"Come to me, all you who are weary and burdened, and I will give you rest. Take my yoke upon you and learn from me, for I am gentle and humble in heart, and you will find rest for your souls. For my yoke is easy and my burden is light."*

Jesus gives the 4 steps here too. 1. Come, 2. Learn – the yoke is another way of saying teaching, then relationship, 3 Learn <u>from</u> me- this is an ongoing refining of relationship, obedience and gaining knowledge straight from hearing the voice of God followed by acting upon what Jesus has revealed to you. 4. Then embrace rest and experience peace.

What I found in explaining this process to people in the hospital setting was that they recognized themselves in this situation. I did not have to convince them, I only had to show them the points of disconnection. Peter starts with the relationship, then the choosing to embrace virtue and move forward in a positive way. Then he adds learning what you do not know, then application, then the process of refinement in perseverance.

The result is critical. You experience goodness, kindness and love, and the process is complete.

The message my patients got so often on their own was that their inner despair and hopelessness was changeable from within themselves. Those feelings were and always are a telltale sign that you have disconnected from God somewhere in the process on these 4 points. Sometimes you lack knowledge, sometimes you lack discipline, sometimes you have disconnected from the source of all truth- Father God, and insight has vanished.

> **Love comes from inside you.**

It is fixable at any point. You can start from step one, choose to connect to God, plug in and gain wisdom and start doing what He shows you to do. It was always a wonderful thing to see by Sunday evening as I was doing my last groups, that the lights in people's eyes were coming on and hope was being birthed.

When it comes to love, it is easy to blame others for your lack of feeling loved. You may be being treated poorly indeed, and many were. But love comes from inside you. Once you act in true love towards another, no one can take that away from you. But if you are acting in selfish self-centeredness then you will be empty inside and nothing and no one can fill that void for you.

It's a choosing to embrace love. And that choice makes all the difference in your world.

Questions to Consider:

Are there areas in your life that you have disconnected from God?

When you do things for others is it conditional?

Do you hope for a return of appreciation and affection?

> Or are your actions conditional with strings attached?

> Do others say that you give with strings attached?

> Are they accurate? How can you know?

Name 5 ways you ask for what you want, desire, need, and care to have.

Do you have the right to ask for such things?

Have you ever felt hopelessness?

Have you ever felt unloved?

Describe that feeling in a group. Explore it in relationship to these insights.

Have you ever expressed love for someone that did not love you back?

> Did they ever come around?

> Did you ever stop loving them?

> Did you give up on them?

Name at least 2 times when you loved someone that was difficult to love and they came around.

Do you have to be loved back in order to love someone?

List 10 ways you give unconditional love.

What would Jesus do?

What's Love Got to Do with It?
Health, Happiness, Long Life.

One of the greatest pleasures of my life was to have been a good friend to a holocaust survivor, Father Kruk of Oakland. He often reminded me that he and Pope John Paul went to the same school in Poland, though a few years apart. He used to tell me stories of the concentration camps and how he survived by keeping a positive attitude. He was selected out of a line for the gas chambers because he could fix furniture. He often spoke of how important it was to forgive, love, and remain positive always, stating that despair would be the last thing you would feel, then you would die. He often spoke of his faith in God and doing good to others. Without those things he says he would have died there.

Another recent story of another survivor (actually 3 such survivors) is told in the documentary. *"The Lady In Number 6: Music Saved My Life"*. It tells the story of Alice Herz-Sommer, a pianist who

Having a healthy perspective on love is essential to happiness, and happiness is essential to health and longevity.

was the world's oldest Holocaust survivor. She discussed the importance of music, laughter, and how to have an optimistic outlook on life. Herz (1903–2014) died at the age of 110.[iii]

Her friend in the documentary sums it up best as she lay dying among 300 corpses. Her comment was, "It never occurred to me that I could be one of them." "Survival is a matter of attitude." She goes on to describe that she never felt like a victim, she did not take it personally and that she "just happened to be here." She states further, "When you were really down in the hell and you come up again, you have learned what matters in life, and what doesn't, and what matters is very few things. Life matters and human relationships, and that's about it. The rest is not important."

Having a healthy perspective on love is essential to happiness. That said, happiness is essential to health and longevity. In the story above, which you can catch by Googling online or catching on Netflix, Alice describes how music makes her happy. It is the thing that brought her Joy. She never hated, always kept her heart full of love. Guards would stop and listen beneath the windows to her playing, and would comment to her later how that gave them hope in such a dark place of hopelessness.

Marriage is often the closest expression of love that many experience. Likewise it often has the greatest opportunity for loss or betrayal. So many of you are looking at this book as a key to finding or experiencing a lasting love relationship within your marriage relationship. I quoted a series of studies on the correlation of longevity and happiness as related to long term marriage relationships in my book "**Your Marriage as God Imagined**..." There is a multitude of studies which show an amazing positive relationship between health, longevity and a balanced, loving, long term "Marriage Relationship."

Here is a quote from that book:
Marriage is now and has always been the healthiest choice for men and women. Many recent studies have shown it leads to greater expressions of happiness and fulfillment. For the skeptics, I will give support materials at the end of the book in Appendix 3, but here is a brief summary of what a massive 17 nation study showed: . "A multiple regression analysis determined that the relationship between marital status and happiness holds in 16 of the 17 nations…Being married was 3.4 times more closely tied to the variance in happiness than was cohabitation, and marriage increases happiness equally among men and women."[iv]

This study, along with many other sources, demonstrates that marriage is still the most viable relationship experience. Married people are:

- *More likely to live longer*
- *More likely to be physically healthier*
- *More likely to be mentally healthier*
- *More likely to be happier*
- *Recover from illness quicker and more successfully*
- Generally, take better care of themselves and avoid risky behavior. [v]

You might question it. Many fight it. Our society is constantly trying to change it. Yet all the data still points in that same direction. Monogamy does work and it is an inescapable reality to the human race and how we are genetically predisposed (Designed) to be.

> Marriage is still the most viable relationship experience

For all our effort in so many different directions, it is amazing to me that we do not devote more time to these realities that are so inescapable. The nature of mankind is to love. There is a shadow nature too, that pulls us in a thousand different directions away from true love. That shadow nature I discuss more in my book **"Living the Authentic Life".**

As a therapist I have sat in hundreds of groups and posed the question to thousands of patients, from people that have worked on high voltage relay stations to the White House, from the proverbial housewife to the multi-millionaire, from the highly religious to those with no concept of God or morality. Out of over six thousand patients, only five have ever said anything different than what I am about to share with you. If you do the math that is less than .01%. If I were to do that as a scientific experiment the results would be astounding. It could be compared to the Law of Gravity or the speed of light.

WHAT IS THE QUESTION?

In its simplest form the question is, "What is life?" The answer is invariably "Love". I ask people to think of themselves one year out, five years out, ten years out, and then imagine themselves at the age of 80.

FRAMING:

What if everything just started working out a little better for you each day. Today gets a little better than yesterday. Next week gets a little better than the few weeks prior. Next month better than the ones before. Before long you notice that you're feeling better. Some of that pain you had been so oppressed by in the past is suddenly not as noticeable.

THE QUESTION OF LIFE:

What would you **'want'** (or desire) that picture to look like. This is not a lottery question. This is not a miracle question, this is not a question of attracting things to myself. I am just asking, what is in your heart, not your head. What does your heart want to have in that picture? At one year? At five years? At ten years?

Ultimately when you're 80 years old and sitting on your proverbial front porch in your rocker and looking around yourself, what is there? What does that picture look like? What is a deal breaker if it is not in that picture? And, what will you be strongly disappointed in if it is still in that picture?

THE ANSWER OF LOVE:

People always describe some form of a loving, long term relationship with a mate and family around them, in a setting of peace. Some include security in job, vocation, health and overcoming long term ailments or addiction issues. A small percentage include the accomplishment of goals and certain achievements of life-long dreams that have been an expression of their inmost strengths. Only 5 people described being completely alone miles away from anyone. Yet even they describe being at peace, relatively healthy, and in good relationship with people they might have to deal with and know.

As a health care professional, it became apparent that significant time needs to be devoted to addressing this important issue of recognizing, building, and maintaining real, lasting, loving relationships.

We either thrive or die by the nature of these relationships. Further, it is possible to have a loving relationship and not recognize it, or even to falsely accuse the one doing the loving of being selfish and evil. This would be an abused person, the one doing the accusing now becoming the abuser.

It is possible to be receiving a loving relationship and simply take it for granted and never invest back into it, leaving it lopsided and unbalanced. This person is running the risk of one day coming home and finding his mate has fled and moved off with their mutual best friend.

It is also possible to believe that you are that loving, kind, wonderful person but be fully using your loved ones and slowly burning those relationships to the ground in a works oriented, codependent relationship. The later would be about 35% of all my patients in the mental hospital. These people generally complain the most about their mental distresses. They make extensive lists of how unhappy they are and will answer the last question on my inventory, "What do you believe about yourself?" Their answer will always be "I am a loving, kind, giving, caring, individual that is not being loved in return." Something is wrong with that picture. We will explore this more in chapter 8 when discussing codependency.

Let's get back to the original question and answer. As I said this is a life question. It could be answered in a thousand ways. Think about it a moment. We spend money on so many things every week. From clothes and groceries to rent and the lawn care, from gadgets to jewelry. But what do we spend on love? How much of your energy do you spend on communicating that love to those you "love" the most? One might argue that all that stuff is an expression of love, but I am not so sure. When that wife buys herself a ring or piece of jewelry for the 100th time or the husband that chili cheese dog or that new iPad, I don't think that really communicates love.

It gets back to the original question and how we framed it. The question comes from the heart not the head. The heart is the deeper part of our brain "the amygdala." Although love is a series of interactions of specific parts of the brain, the generally accepted area is the amygdala. It is safe to say that if the amygdala is damaged, then your love relationships will be suffering as well. I say this here to let you know that there is significant science and biology involved here. We are not just talking about fuzzy ideas that cannot be defined or have no particular meaning. We are created to love and our own biology testifies to this fact. Love is a real thing that can be measured within the brain and scientists are studying this daily.

Think about it for a moment. What happens when someone gets rejected or perhaps betrayed in a serious relationship? They feel many things don't they? Let me rephrase this. What happened to you the last time you were treated in such a way by someone that was supposed to 'have your back?'

You felt that sting of betrayal, loss, grief, anger, sadness, and anxiety. This is just part of life, right? Sure it is. However, take that feeling, keep remembering it, now amplify that feeling just a bit and stretch it out for several months, then perhaps several years. Now that is a condition that begins to affect all your relationships and your health. You begin a trek of long term depression or anxiety that affects your central nervous system, your blood chemistry, your brain chemistry, all your relationships, your activities, and on it goes.

You close yourself off to certain relationships believing they will only disappoint. You stop many activities as they no longer satisfy, and you spend more time alone and in front of the TV. You start a new story line of what you tell yourself about the world and how you relate to it, one that is more negative, less inspiring and certainly less trusting.

As a health care professional, I have worked telephonically now for several years talking with thousands of adults at all ages of life, from Hawaii to Maine, from Florida to Canada. It is a proven medical fact that when people go through traumatic events, deal with chronic conditions of health issues or stressful situations, they are twice as likely to suffer depression and prolonged anxiety. In this state they are 3 times more likely to suffer greater serious health issues that will often lead to higher incidences of emergency room visits and hospital admissions. Often depression sets in and a cascade of circumstances begin a downward trend.

There is a lot of science to this that is statistically proven, so much so that the health care industry is investing millions of their capital profits back into the system in order to change what is happening to people. The shift is moving from an insurance company simply paying your bill to proactively trying to change your life for the better. What is the motivation of the insurance companies? Money! They want you alive and healthy for a very-very long time, paying that premium. If you are healthy, that is money in their pockets.

> **Love focuses on the positive.**

In my work with one insurance company we estimated that my work gave a positive impact and changed the lives of 25,000 people. All from a positive phone call in a short term solution focused relationship that took an average of 8 calls. We call it co-morbidity. My job as a health care professional has been to provide a point of contact to intervene and encourage positive mood and health changes.

But what does this have to do with love? Love focuses on the positive. Allow me to quote here from a paper I read some time ago by Matthieu Ricard of the Mind and Life Institute and Michael Dambrun of Clermont University. In Ricard's work on altruism he contrasts the western culture's strong focus on the negative with studies showing results of health and longevity by focusing on the positive and what he calls altruistic, heart felt actions to help others.

"Since the early 1990s, the movement of positive psychology has attempted to correct this imbalance by promoting the study of the conditions and processes which contribute to the optimal functioning of individuals, groups and institutions (Gable & Haidt, 2005; Seligman & Csikszentmihalyi, 2000). From this point of view, the study of well-being and happiness has gradually become a field of primary importance (e.g., Csikszentmihalyi & Hunter, 2003; Diener, 2000; Lyubomirsky, Sheldon, & Schakde, 2005). Moreover, a substantial amount of research has been done in this field, making it possible to identify several factors implicated in the regulation of these phenomena (e.g., Ryan & Deci, 2001; Veenhoven, 1997)."[vi]

> **When was the last time you went to the counselor to affair proof your marriage?**

The imbalance they are speaking of here is the western culture's focus on the negative. Think about it for a moment. Do you go to the doctor for a wellness visit? Many don't. When you get medical screenings, they are looking for the negatives. Your doctor treats you for the negatives, high blood pressure or blood sugars, or cholesterol. We wish to fix what's broken, correct what's wrong and never give attention to what is good or right. You're doing good in a particular area, great, "keep it up," end of discussion.

You get told to go to a counselor to do what? Fix a broken relationship, fix a broken heart, or a damaged spirit, or a wounded soul. When was the last time you went to the counselor to affair proof your marriage or to turn your dull conversations into lively, stimulating, wildly exciting adventures?

You don't. That is because it is a western cultural mindset. But it is changing. The whole industry is changing from fixing broken health systems to creating healthier systems, socially, physically, mentally, and even spiritually. These are all included in standard screenings and treatment plans and the movement is growing into industry and also into the corporate world of the workforce.

Why? It is a massive shifting of focus into you being healthier and living healthier for longer and longer periods of time. The day will come when running a marathon at ninety is a common thing. People will die of old age and not so much from the many diseases typically associated with old age.

What all this has to do with your love life is that it is exposing a great deal of research and data that is showing just how important healthy, loving relationships are to overall health and long life.

In the paper quoted above they use the term **"authentic-durable happiness."** They maintain, as Richard does in all his writings on compassion and authenticity, that "selflessness" is the key to authentic-durable happiness. Richard equates this selflessness as the ability to place yourself in another's shoes and have compassion and genuine concern or love for them. Then to devote time to relieving the pain, distress, or afflictions of others in altruistic actions on the behalf of others. Here is another quote from their conclusion: **"We argue that our psychological functioning is determined by the structure of the self, and that authentic happiness can be obtained when selflessness, rather than self-centeredness, occurs."**

What does this have to do with love? Absolutely – Everything! For the Christian, that should resonate with a sound of familiarity. Jesus said, "Do unto others as you would have them do unto you."

LOVE CAN SAVE YOUR LIFE:

You really want to pay attention here, especially if you feel stressed!!

One of the things I really like doing is to watch a program called TED Talks. **TED (Technology, Entertainment and Design)** is a global set of conferences run by a private non-profit foundation, under the slogan "Ideas Worth Spreading". As you might imagine from the title there are teachers, professors, doctors and PH.D.s, inventors, leaders, scientists, craftsmen, artists of every kind from all over the globe presenting their research, ideas, and experience in a 19 minute presentation. One such presentation is the primary resource of the following material. The speaker has done her homework and given a collection of facts dealing with her research on stress, building resilience, the role of oxytocin, the importance of deep meaningful social connection, and how altruism can actually, really and truly **save your life.**

Kelly McGonigal is a psychologist that has given a great TED Talk. Oxytocin, an important neuro-hormone, is known as the cuddle hormone due to it being released when you hug someone. Just a six second hug will release enough oxytocin in your system to change your brain and body chemistry. So will shaking hands, looking at baby pictures of any kind, and walking among trees and green grass. However its greatest production is in interactions with other human beings. The more direct interaction, the greater the release of this neuro-hormone, the greater your resilience and strengthening of your physical and emotional systems. It motivates you to have closer contact with close friends and family. It also increases your capacity for empathy and the ability to care for others. Further, the heart has built in receptors that respond to oxytocin which stimulates the heart, promoting healing and strengthening it.

McGonigal quotes a study of 1000 people tracked for 5 years. The result of the study showed that a major stress event can increase your chances of dying by 30%. This is not much of a surprise to all us health care professionals who have been training people for years to *reduce stress*. However there was one amazing fact that emerged from this study. It showed that people who stayed connected and involved in helping friends and neighbors, stress had *NO EFFECT* on health or mortality whatsoever. So it is fair to say that if you stay connected in helping others—an act of love-- that you will eliminate your chances of being killed by a stressful event. Another way of looking at it is that you reduce your chances of dying prematurely by 30%. [vii]

Wow, now that is significant isn't it? I am reminded of one woman I worked with for a few months. She was a living illustration of this study. She was a recent widow with a major health issue. My concern was that her recent life event of becoming a widow and this health issue would set her up for depression or even death. Remember that her chances of death have just increased 30%. In working with her, I discovered that she had a hobby. She would make baby gowns and baby receiving blankets for newborns at the local hospitals for underprivileged mothers that did not have the resources for such things. What a precious gift.

I inquired as to how long it took, how many years she had been doing it, and the average number of blankets she actually makes every month doing this wonderful deed. I calculated the number of mothers and children she had touched over the several years she had been doing this. It turns out she had ministered directly to over 800 families. At that time it would have been actually 1600 considering mother and child. And it will keep giving into the future as those blankets will most likely be passed down and be used by mothers to come for their children.

In creating receiving blankets this dear woman was also receiving much needed oxytocin that would keep her brain, heart and body healthy for years to come.

It is therefore no great surprise that long term relationships that have intrinsically deep and meaningful connections show a direct relationship to a much healthier, happier, and longer life. McGonigal concludes with an amazing remark in her talk that I completely agree with and have heard in many other venues. "One thing we know for certain is that chasing meaning is better for your health than avoiding discomfort." Her final thought is to go after whatever it is that creates meaning in your life. [viii]

The other amazing aspect of her talk is that she reveals a study done on the attitude or belief of stress itself. The study looked at those who simply felt stressed (low to highly) and believed that stress was really bad for them, contrasted with the groups that felt stressed (low to highly) and did not believe that stress was particularly bad for them. Then they simply looked at who died and who did not within 5 years. The result might amaze you. It did McGonigal, as well as me.

The group that believed that stress was particularly harmful for them experienced a higher death rate of 43%. That is a scientific statistic showing a 43% more likelihood to die, not from stress, but from a belief.

> All attitude is seated in things we believe to be true about our lives and the way we relate to the world around us.

The longer I live as a Christian and the longer I attempt to help people as a Clinical Health Care Professional, the more I see this profound relationship to attitude. All attitude is seated in things we believe to be true about our lives and the way we relate to the world around us.

Solomon taught in Proverbs 23:7, *"For as he thinketh in his heart, so is he"*, and in Prov. 4:23 *"Above all else, guard your heart, for everything you do flows from it."*

Jesus taught the importance of beliefs flowing from the heart. In Jesus' teachings we see a direct link to worry and anxiety tied to darkness and actually destroying the body as well as the spirit. In fact in Matt 6 he connects worry, unforgiveness, stress, and anxiety, to our thought processes that lead us to unfulfillment and even to our own destruction. Jesus is adamant on the importance of belief and inner peace, and that they are within our control.

Matt. 15:18 "But the things that come out of a person's mouth come from the heart, and these defile them."

Matt. 6:19-23, 31-34 "Do not store up for yourselves treasures on earth, where moths and vermin destroy, and where thieves break in and steal. But store up for yourselves treasures in heaven, where moths and vermin do not destroy, and where thieves do not break in and steal. For where your treasure is, there your heart will be also. "The eye is the lamp of the body. If your eyes are healthy, your whole body will be full of light. But if your eyes are unhealthy, your whole body will be full of darkness. If then the light within you is darkness, how great is that darkness!"

"So do not worry, saying, 'What shall we eat?' or 'What shall we drink?' or 'What shall we wear?' For the pagans run after all these things, and your heavenly Father knows that you need them. But seek first his kingdom and his righteousness, and all these things will be given to you as well. Therefore, do not worry about tomorrow, for tomorrow will worry about itself. Each day has enough trouble of its own."

Questions to ask yourself:

What are you stressed about?

Do you feel like stress is taking a heavy toll on your life?

Do you believe that stress can build your life?

List your 5 greatest stressors in life.

List 3 things your stress is keeping you from doing what you want.

Name 5 ways to destress your life.

Do you believe that serving others in love can save your life?

List 5 ways that you can serve others with joy.

List the 5 greatest ways that you served someone in the past.

How did this change your perspective?

Imagine a Culture Without Love

Many might argue today that such societies are a thing of the past. However, our modern, or current literature is full of books and movies of real people telling real stories of just such societies. Many tell of living in a society that one day was a kind of utopia then suddenly over a few months or even days, turned into complete hatred and destruction. Let us consider a few societies that have demonstrated a profound lack of love in recent history.

Recently my wife and I watched a couple of movies of just such times. "Unbroken" depicts the harsh atrocities of WWII with Japan and the treatment of allied soldiers in prisoner of war camps. We also watched a documentary from the other side of the world on Winston Churchill and the incredibly courageous people of England surviving the bombing "Blitz" of WWII. We do not have to look far or ask too many questions to see picture after picture of millions of victims slaughtered simply because of race. We could also give many current examples today of killing, intolerance, and inhumane treatment of our fellow man. Just watch your TV news channel.

When we think of a society as demonstrating a profound lack of love, we immediately have to define those terms. What is a lack of love?

We can look at Hitler and the German Nazi New World Order. They oversaw and implemented the relentless murder of millions of innocent people for the sake of pure hatred. We can look at the third president of Uganda, Idi Amin and say here is a dictatorship that showed great cruelty and certainly a lack of love for many people that he oversaw the slaughter of. Names like Ruanda conjure up mass slaughter and killings for any and every reason by ordinary people.

That's the extreme. How about a society that just practices ostracization and mutual exclusion. You may not be directly persecuted, but you are just never welcome and you are shut out. For many this is a daily experience in life, for Christians living in Islamic states, for the refugees of war, famine, and disasters this is their plight. They will be foreigners caught in intractable situations, often due to no fault of their own. Sometimes they are there due to an attempt to find a better life, only to find isolation, loneliness, and hardship.

One lady I counseled with recently was of the Philippine nationality and had come to Canada for a new life. She was a foreigner in a strange land. Her husband had given up and gone back to the Philippines, taking the children with him. She was alone and finding her job to be increasingly oppressive. It seemed to her that no one would give her a break. She felt desperate and ready to give up. No one was showing her love. Perhaps she just did not know where to look for it. Perhaps she was a victim of circumstance. She felt alone even though she was surrounded by people.

So one of the first things we notice about love and the experience of love is that sense that we are not alone, and the opposite is true as well. When societies or groups of people decide that it is us against everyone else, they begin to isolate, separate, segregate, discriminate, manipulate, use, abuse, dominate, and control others. These are the descriptors of a lack of love.

I like to simplify those descriptors to just four words; **use, manipulation, domination, and control**. I have always found in every relationship whether individual or corporate that when I find these descriptors at work they are driven by self-centered ambition that seeks profit or fulfillment at the expense of others. The design of selfish ambition is to take advantage of others in order to fulfill one's own agenda with an expressed disregard for the other person or persons.

There is a movement afoot in the Western world that believes this is the very purpose of mankind. Simplified it is the 'dog eat dog' mentality. It is a perversion of Darwin's theories of evolution. Some think and live on the premise that the strong should survive and exploit everything and everyone possible in order to gain the slightest advantage, even future generations.

This then becomes a society without love. It is a world meant to advantage only one, the one at the top. Who has the most money or power? Anyone and everyone below that one is a potential target and resource meant only to serve the one in power. That sounds exactly like Kim Jong Un, who regularly executes his cabinet members when he doesn't like them any longer.

While we hear thousands of these stories we also hear of the stories within those horrific events. There are stories of people putting their lives on the line to rescue, to shelter, to defend, and to comfort those who were being treated so unjustly. We see stories of light within the great darkness. Yes light. Anyone that was touched by such acts of kindness describes that person showing grace and goodness to them describe it as light to them.

As a counselor I speak with people daily that are in tough situations. They are perplexed about how to feel about others and even how to feel about themselves. Do they believe the really bad things others are saying to them about themselves? Do they lean into and accept the darkness or fight back with light? Some are in marriages, some are living with a partner, and some are in difficult situations where they simply feel exploited.

Have you ever been invited to a friend's home for dinner? They treated you really special and then told you to just stay there while they cleaned the table. Then they brought out the Tupperware, the Amway, or some other pyramid product scheme? You realize that you have just been used. These people tend to burn through all their friendships in order to reach a personal and corporate goal. They wish to become that one at the top, get the diamond ring, the special car, and lots of money. What you realize, though you may not frame it this way right off is that, they do not love you, rather they are using you, and it does not feel good.

In a society without love we see people exploited, subjugated, treated poorly, even killed for any and every reason. There is a profound lack of love. It is selfish ambition at its zenith. But most of us live in a different kind of world. Most of us experience a different kind of exclusion and subtle discriminations. These can be over race and color of our skin, cultural background, religion or lack of belief, college associations, male or female, rich or poor, east or west Texas, and many other things we discriminate over. It is impossible to be human and not do this. Where it is wrong is when we find ourselves taking away someone's rights, limiting their choices, and in some way diminishing their dignity. Such actions will always have a distinct motivation behind them of selfish self-centered ambition to elevate one at the expense of another.

The nature and structure of the New Testament is such that it defines principles of love and how any and all people calling themselves followers of Christ are to destroy any such attitudes or behaviors. A quick look into the heart of the Apostle James shows us a picture of how ministers in the New Testament viewed selfish self-centeredness. James 3:13-18

"Who is wise and understanding among you? Let them show it by their good life, by deeds done in the humility that comes from wisdom. But if you harbor bitter envy and selfish ambition in your hearts, do not boast about it or deny the truth. Such "wisdom" does not come down from heaven but is earthly, unspiritual, demonic. For where you have envy and selfish ambition, there you find disorder and every evil practice. But the wisdom that comes from heaven is first of all pure; then peace-loving, considerate, submissive, full of mercy and good fruit, impartial and sincere. Peacemakers who sow in peace reap a harvest of righteousness."

James 2:1-7 "My brothers and sisters, believers in our glorious Lord Jesus Christ must not show favoritism. Suppose a man comes into your meeting wearing a gold ring and fine clothes, and a poor man in filthy old clothes also comes in. If you show special attention to the man wearing fine clothes and say, "Here's a good seat for you," but say to the poor man, "You stand there" or "Sit on the floor by my feet," have you not discriminated among yourselves and become judges with evil thoughts?

Listen, my dear brothers and sisters: Has not God chosen those who are poor in the eyes of the world to be rich in faith and to inherit the kingdom he promised those who love him? But you have dishonored the poor. Is it not the rich who are exploiting you? Are they not the ones who are dragging you into court? Are they not the ones who are blaspheming the noble name of him to whom you belong?"

Compare and contrast such cultures with the Golden rule; ***Matthew 7:12 "So in everything, do to others what you would have them do to you, for this sums up the Law and the Prophets."*** In this we see the heart of love and the heart of what it means to care for our fellow man.

DISCERNING THE LIGHT AND DARKNESS: SUBTLETIES OF LOVE

"This is the message we have heard from him and declare to you:

God is light; in him there is no darkness at all."

1 John 1:5

"Dear friends, let us love one another, for love comes from God.

Everyone who loves has been born of God and knows God."

1 John 4:7

THERE ARE TWO STATEMENTS IN THE BIBLE THAT GIVE A DESCRIPTION OF GOD THAT I WANT TO HIGHLIGHT HERE; "GOD IS LIGHT," AND "GOD IS LOVE."

When people describe that light, they are describing hope as seen in acts of love and grace given in a self-sacrificing way. These ideas and concepts are completely interwoven and tied to freedom and the Christian life throughout the New Testament.

To live in love is to give off light. Light is always associated with health, growth, hope, encouragement, good works, enlightenment, revelation, a future, happiness, joy, love, and peace. Darkness is of course the opposite. Darkness is associated with sickness, disease, despair, depression, discouragement, being overcome, ignorance, evil deeds, and being stuck in hopelessness. Let's look at some scriptures that give a more complete picture of this connection:

"God, the blessed and only Ruler, the King of kings and Lord of lords, who alone is immortal and who lives in unapproachable light," 1 Tim. 6:16

"He reveals deep and hidden things; he knows what lies in darkness, and light dwells with him." Daniel 2:22

"Whoever does not love does not know God, because God is love." 1 John 4:8, 16

"Dear friends, let us love one another, for love comes from God. Everyone who loves has been born of God and knows God." 1 John 4:7

"Greater love has no one than this: to lay down one's life for one's friends." John 15:13

"I am the good shepherd. The good shepherd lays down his life for the sheep" John 10:11

"You are the light of the world. A city set on a hill cannot be hidden; nor does anyone light a lamp and put it under a basket, but on the lampstand, and it gives light to all who are in the house. "Let your light shine before men in such a way that they may see your good works, and glorify your Father who is in heaven. Matt. 5:14-16

"So that you may become blameless and pure, "children of God without fault in a warped and crooked generation." Then you will shine among them like stars in the sky" Philippians 2:15

"In the beginning was the Word, and the Word was with God, and the Word was God. He was with God in the beginning. Through him all things were made; without him nothing was made that has been made. In him was life, and that life was the light of all mankind. The light shines in the darkness, and the darkness has not overcome it.

There was a man sent from God whose name was John. He came as a witness to testify concerning that light, so that through him all might believe. He himself was not the light; (John the Baptist), he came only as a witness to the light.

The true light that gives light to everyone was coming into the world. He was in the world, and though the world was made through him, the world did not recognize him. He came to that which was his own, but his own did not receive him. Yet to all who did receive him, to those who believed in his name, he gave the right to become children of God, children born not of natural descent, nor of human decision or a husband's will, but born of God. The Word became flesh and made his dwelling among us. We have seen his glory, the glory of the one and only Son, who came from the Father, full of grace and truth." John 1:1-14

Light and love are linked together. They are linked to acts of kindness, acts of grace, hope, acceptance and inclusion, non-judgmentalism, provision and encouragement. So the opposite is also true. When we see hope being diminished, exclusion as the rule, disapproval as the norm, selfish self-centeredness, lack of compassion, legalism and the lack of grace for others replaced by a selective entitlement for a few at the expense of others, with harshness ruling, then we see a lack of love. In fact, in those cases it is the opposite of love. The Bible has a term for this in the book of James, selfish ambition. In Matthew Rickard's book on Altruism he calls it selfish self-centeredness.

Why should this be important? Aside from the obvious of a society being a very dark and hopeless place to live, it is important in discerning when the opposite of love is being given or received as we explore in chapters to come. We look at the question, "Am I being loving in my relationships," as well as, "Is someone else being loving in their relationship with me?" by examining whether I am bringing light, encouragement, hope, and opportunity for growth to someone or to myself in my actions. Also vise-versa, are their actions doing that for me?

> **Light and love are linked together.**

One of my life mentors, a man I shall always look up to and respect, did something to me that I had difficulty interpreting at the time. I worked for him during the first year of our relationship. During that year he could have given me a raise and did not. I asked him about it and he passed it off somehow at the time. Now this was during a time that my family desperately needed me to make a living, and working for Dean was our only means of support. Dean's actions and decision to pass me over had a deep effect, with the perception of the darkness of disapproval even though I worked very-very hard to win respect and approval. It cast a shadow of darkness that gave cause for doubt and unbelief. During the second year I struck out on my own and started my own business. We stayed friends and I never faulted him for not blessing me. Yet I knew in my spirit that his action was not based in love.

Fast forward 20 years into the future and I am visiting Dean. I start discussing the nature of our relationship and discussed that time and why he passed me over for a raise when he gave others a raise. He confessed that he did it purposefully due to the actions of another employee who was my supervisor at that time. He discussed how that fellow (who has since passed) used to cheat him on the time by taking extra-long lunches and that is why he did not give me a raise. He assumed since I worked under this man, I must be guilty of the same. I assured him that I was not, and that I often confronted that guy about his actions and would refuse to go to lunch with him for that reason. Dean apologized and said he should have discussed this with me and given me an honest chance to represent myself instead of making a judgement. He told me how much he actually respected me and my wife for being such a hard working couple that never faltered, and how he admired how well we had done in raising our daughters to be such women of God. It took 20 years for the light to be turned on fully in this relationship.

This is the kind of subtly that creeps into many relationships. It creeps into societal norms as well, shaping private and public opinions and eventually policy that affects people in dramatic ways. Though Dean and I remained great friends until his death a few years ago, this event illustrates how a single act can bring discouragement and darkness in a time of need. It's not that Dean meant to hurt me, rather he simply believed something that was not true of me and acted in judgement rather than encouragement in that action towards me. Don't get me wrong here, later Dean would do many things to bless me and come along side of me as our relationship progressed. I will always have a profound gratitude for his friendship and blessing in my life.

I am reminded of one such event in scriptures that also illustrates this in a slightly different way. In this story there was a woman whose life was saved by doing good. Read on in Acts 9: 36-*41 "In Joppa there was a disciple named Tabitha (in Greek her name is Dorcas); she was always doing good and helping the poor. About that time she became sick and died, and her body was washed and placed in an upstairs room. Lydda was near Joppa; so when the disciples heard that Peter was in Lydda, they sent two men to him and urged him, "Please come at once!" Peter went with them, and when he arrived he was taken upstairs to the room. All the widows stood around him, crying and showing him the robes and other clothing that Dorcas had made while she was still with them. Peter sent them all out of the room; then he got down on his knees and prayed. Turning toward the dead woman, he said, "Tabitha, get up." She opened her eyes, and seeing Peter she sat up. He took her by the hand and helped her to her feet. Then he called for the believers, especially the widows, and presented her to them alive."*

In this story, doing well to others extends beyond the grave. Of course Jesus taught that we should be about doing good to others always. Matt. 7:12 *"In everything, therefore, treat people the same way you want them to treat you, for this is the Law and the Prophets."* Paul also taught this in many other scriptures in the New Testament.

Questions to Consider:

Have you ever been in a social situation that was devoid of Love? Describe that situation and the feelings associated with it.

Describe a culture without love. What would be going on there?

Share with the group stories from your past that have been devoid of love towards you.

Have you ever left a job, a close friend, or a church and never spoken with anyone from that relationship again?

It may be the opposite too, did they shun you and cast you out?

Describe to someone what that felt like.

Perhaps it still feels that way.

The Unraveling of Love

This chapter deals with love in two directions. First, codependency slowly breaking love relationships down and replacing authentic love with a twisted entanglement. This is the first direction of dealing with the passive aggressive distortion. The second direction we look at is how to untangle love from those strongholds of codependency and the passive aggressive control that inhibits one from experiencing true love. We look at how one gets free of codependency and how to once again give and receive authentic love.

I was first confronted with this issue in grad school working on my first master's degree in Marriage and Family Therapy. My professor posed the question for a paper we were to write and it just didn't set well with my existing theology. She asked "How do you get your way?" My first response was "What? As Christians we are not supposed to get our way!" Her response was, "Why not? If you don't get your way, who is getting their way? Is it a healthy family system where no one gets their way? Is that reasonable or even possible?"

You may argue that Jesus taught selflessness and doing good to others. But is that all that Jesus taught? Did Jesus teach other things as well related to getting your way? More important, how did Jesus live and conduct his ministry and life?

Consider these things about Jesus. Jesus did get his way often. Here are just 11 examples of Jesus getting his way.

Overturning the money tables: Matt 21:12 *"Jesus entered the temple courts and drove out all who were buying and selling there. He overturned the tables of the money changers and the benches of those selling doves."*

Sending out the 70, giving them commands: *Luke 10 "After this the Lord appointed seventy-two[a] others and sent them two by two ahead of him to* every town and place where he was about to go. ² He told them, **"The harvest is plentiful, but the workers are few."**

Jesus ordering servants to bring him water pots, then turning water into new wine: *John 2:7 "Jesus said to the servants, "Fill the jars with water"; so they filled them to the brim."*

How about Jesus healing on the Sabbath: *Luke 13:14 "Indignant because Jesus had healed on the Sabbath, the synagogue leader said to the people, "There are six days for work. So come and be healed on those days, not on the Sabbath."*

Jesus walking on water, then calling Peter to come to him: *Matt. 14:29 "Come," he said. Then Peter got down out of the boat, walked on the water and came toward Jesus."*

Jesus commanding the 5,000 to sit down, commanding the disciples to feed them, and multiplying the loaves and fish: *Matt. 14:13-21; Mark 6:30-44; Luke 9:10-17 "Jesus said, "Have the people sit down." There was plenty of grass in that place, and they sat down (about five thousand men were there). Jesus then took the loaves, gave thanks, and distributed to those who were seated as much as they wanted. He did the same with the fish."*

Jesus commanding that we love each other: *John 13:34-5 "A new command I give you: Love one another. As I have loved you, so you must love one another. By this everyone will know that you are my disciples, if you love one another."*

Jesus standing in the gap for the woman about to be stoned to death: *John 8:5-10 "When they kept on questioning him, he straightened up and said to them, "Let any one of you who is without sin be the first to throw a stone at her."*

Jesus' command to follow him by keeping his commands: *John 14:23-4 "Jesus replied, "Anyone who loves me will obey my teaching. My Father will love them, and we will come to them and make our home with them. Anyone who does not love me will not obey my teaching. These words you hear are not my own; they belong to the Father who sent me."*

Jesus inviting the rich young ruler to follow him: *Mark 10:21 "Jesus looked at him and loved him. "One thing you lack," he said. "Go, sell everything you have and give to the poor, and you will have treasure in heaven."* Then come, follow me." If the rich young ruler was to get his way, he would have kept his money and followed Jesus. But that did not happen.

<u>Jesus inviting the disciples to follow him:</u> Mark 1:16-18 *"As He was going along by the Sea of Galilee, He saw Simon and Andrew, the brother of Simon, casting a net in the sea; for they were fishermen. And Jesus said to them, "Follow Me, and I will make you become fishers of men." Immediately they left their nets and followed Him....."*

If you read the New Testament looking for how often Jesus was commanding, asking, or inviting others to do something, then you come away with a totally different picture of Jesus. If Jesus taught us to be like him then I have to deal with my mindset that "Christians are to never ask for anything, expect anything, and or especially never demand anything." To **demand your way** would be most "**un-Christ-like**." Or <u>so I have been taught</u> by this way of thinking all my life.

But now I am seeing it from the Biblical point of view, **nothing could be more un-Christ-like.** <u>We must take a stand for what we want to see happen, believe is right and true, what we need for our life and for others, and especially what we see and hear Father God doing in and around us.</u> Of course we are to always stand for these things. When we consider these points it's obvious.

If the things Jesus did is not getting one's way, then what is? If Jesus gets his way, then what is wrong with you or I getting our way? We are new a new creation created in Christ Jesus, alive and new by the Holy Spirit! We are called to be like him and we are the force of God in the earth advancing the Kingdom of God.

Of course if you are not living for the Kingdom of God and are not following Jesus daily, then there only remains a fearful expectation of judgment and not of promise. Hebrews 10: 19-25, *"Therefore, brothers and sisters, since we have confidence to enter the Most Holy Place by the blood of Jesus, by a new and living way opened for us through the curtain, that is, his body, and since we have a great priest over the house of God, let us draw near to God with a sincere heart and with the full assurance that faith brings, having our hearts sprinkled to cleanse us from a guilty conscience and having our bodies washed with pure water. Let us hold unswervingly to the hope we profess, for he who promised is faithful. And let us consider how we may spur one another on toward love and good deeds, not giving up meeting together, as some are in the habit of doing, but encouraging one another—and all the more as you see the Day approaching. If we deliberately keep on sinning after we have received the knowledge of the truth, no sacrifice for sins is left, but only a fearful expectation of judgment and of raging fire that will consume the enemies of God"*

My Personal Transformation by the Liberation of Love

The paper I had to write in seminary would be a beginning point that would eventually change my mind set, not only about getting my own way in life, marriage, business, and writing, but eventually my entire mindset regarding Kingdom living.

This question of you getting your way strikes at the very heart of how God loves you. If you believe you should never get your way, then you are still believing that God wants to use you for His benefit. Somehow you get lost in his great purposes. Your will and your desires are not important and are to be completely subverted.

Little did I know that when Dr. Wicker asked me this question and I began espousing this doctrine of, "More of Jesus, less of me, all of Jesus, none of me" (actually a quote of Smith Wigglesworth), that it would start a revelation of how I saw Jesus, the Father and the world. It literally overturned everything. Everything had to be overturned if I was going to be used of God to help any one of those 10,000 souls He would place in front of me in the mental hospitals, nationwide telephonic counseling, and five different counseling offices.

My professor's response to my objections was simple. "Everyone needs to get their way. Everyone is important. Everyone is just as important as the next person. When you are counseling someone, it is important to remember that there are no second class individuals. God loves you just like He loves Jesus. There is no distinction." Her words rang a bell that is still ringing true today.

Within eighteen months of that class I would find myself doing group and individual counseling in the mental hospital. These were faith based groups, PTSD soldier's groups, and intensive psychiatric conditions. Of all those patients, I estimate just over 35% of them were dealing with issues so significantly impacting their lives that they either had just attempted to kill themselves, or were there as inpatients because they could not stop wanting to do so.

> "Everyone needs to get their way. Everyone is important. Everyone is just as important as the next person."

Ultimately it all comes down to this issue; Does God love you for what he can get you to do for him, or does God love you for who you are? This is the question in every marriage, in every job, in every relationship, every business, and in every church.

It is a Massive Question? It challenges how you see God, yourself, and your relationship to everyone else. In the end, it comes down to how you define LOVE.

Questions to Consider:

Tell the group, or your close friend, how you get your way.

List 3 ways or things you do to get your way.

>Do you build a case, negotiate, demand, just do it, or wait till everyone has gone out to do what you want to do?

>Do you defer to others on decisions like where to eat out?

Can you articulate exactly what you want, when you want it, and what the consequences will be if you do not get it?

>Ok what are those things?

Are you one that straightens an order out at a restaurant first or complains how messed up the service and order was after the fact?

Do you have the right and responsibility to seek after what you want, need, and or desire?   Is that Godly or self-centered?

Getting Free to Love

There are a few things that can make you stuck in love. Getting stuck seems to be a rather easy thing to do. One might say it is the human condition. Even though our hearts desire it from the core of our being, we still get bogged down frequently and are unhappy. Being discontent is your first indicator that something is wrong in the love department. You may be out of sync in a relationship, in being true to yourself, or in your walk with Father God. This chapter is designed to address the most common reasons people get stuck and how to unstick yourself.

GETTING UNSTUCK FROM CODEPENDENCY AND CARETAKING INSTEAD OF CAREGIVING.

We will start with codependency since I have addressed it as the largest block to love. Of course there have been thousands of books written on the subject and you can Google it and get several helpful lists dealing with caretaking verses caregiving. Being a caretaker is easy to do when you are assuming the role of being someone's caregiver. The bond is a powerful one and very difficult to break.

We see the power of that role in many famous people. Christopher Reeve, known best for his role as Superman, had a tragic accident. "On May 27, 1995, Reeve became a quadriplegic after being thrown from a horse during an equestrian competition in Culpeper, Virginia. He required a wheelchair and a portable ventilator for the rest of his life. "[ix] He was cared for the rest of his life by his devoted wife Dana Morosini. Christopher would die at the age of 52. Dana, his wife would die within a year and a half later of lung cancer at the age of 44, still in the prime of her life.

Another story from our headlines is that of Johnny Cash and wife June Carter Cash. June became ill and died on May 15, 2003at the age of 73. Johnny Cash her husband then dies just 4 short months later at the age of 71.

Many people call this the greatest love, when one cannot live without the other. Perhaps, but for me as a healthcare professional I see it differently. I watched my mother go through the same thing with my father. She doted over my father in his failing health until he passed. Then we had to put her in the hospital for several months with a couple of operations that were long overdue. She had neglected her health as she cared for him so very much.

I have counseled with hundreds of women in the same predicament and helped them navigate the fine balance of love for someone else and care for yourself.

So how do you get free of codependency and being a caretaker instead of a caregiver?

1. Stop doing for someone else what they can do and should do for themselves.
2. Check your need factor. Are you doing for someone else because you need them to need you?
    a. Needing something from someone that they cannot deliver or choose not to give sets you up for a lifetime of constantly seeking approval or appreciation where it is not forthcoming.
3. Stop rescuing, start assisting. Stop trying to fix people, instead offer assistance to help them move toward taking steps to be responsible for their own self-care. Keep your needs, wants, and desires on a near equal basis with others.
4. Seek God's voice and direction. Are you doing something because God told you, or are you doing it out of need or guilt? Ask God to lead you, speak to you, and direct what you should do next. Seek God for the healthiest ways to relate as possible.
5. Help others embrace the consequences of their own choices. Ask yourself, "Am I trying to insulate someone from truth in some way?" Help others embrace their reality and it will help you embrace your own.

6. Are you easily offended? This is a classic sign of codependency. Remember that this is a sign that you are not loving, but judging. In 1 Corinthians 13:5 Paul says that love; **"does not dishonor others, it is not self-seeking, it is not easily angered, it keeps no record of wrongs."** To take offense is to be self-seeking and dishonoring of others. It is a confession of what is in your own heart. Choose to not be offended, to give grace, compassion, understanding, and be longsuffering.
7. Remember that God is your God, but He is also their God too. If you are in God's spot in their life, then you are weakening their ability to depend upon God for their needs, wants, and desires. Stop playing God.
8. Start learning about codependency and caretaking. Get in a class, get in a group, seek out counseling. It is just like learning another language. Have you ever noticed that in your own life? You can say how you feel, what you think, or something you have done or want only to find no one is listening? This means that you have built a relationship of codependent expectation. You are not being heard because you have built that relationship in such a way as to not be heard. Being heard will take time to learn how to speak and establish relationship rules that will allow you to be heard. Jesus made himself heard. They did not like what they heard, but he made himself heard. This takes years to fully learn while unlearning those other unhealthy patterns or relating.
9. If you are in a relationship that someone is codependent upon then you need to change. Take these same steps and turn them around.
    a. Seek God first. Ask God to help you meet your needs without imposing upon others.
    b. Take responsibility for your own needs, wants, desires, and hearing from God.

- c. Stop asking others to do things for you just because it feels good to you.
- d. Ask God "What He wants for others in your life." Remember how Jesus lived: John 5:19 *"Jesus gave them this answer: "Very truly I tell you, the Son can do nothing by himself; he can do only what he sees his Father doing, because whatever the Father does the Son also does."* And John 14:10, *"The words I say to you I do not speak on my own authority. Rather, it is the Father, living in me, who is doing his work."*
- e. Jesus only gave directions and instructions to his bride that the Father gave him to give. It is the greatest thing you can do in any relationship to only ask from others what God the Father is personally telling you to ask for. Everything else is of the flesh and selfish in nature. This may be tough to hear, indeed too tough for many, but it is true. You are commanded to walk like Jesus walked, and this is how he walked.
- f. Work at being more sensitive to the needs of your loved one. Work at being fair, give them what they need and desire even when you must seek it out.
- g. Change the way you relate to your loved one. Seek their needs and desires first. Seek ways you can help them become a smashing success and experience God's love and acceptance completely by giving your love and acceptance completely and unconditionally.

Getting Free of Unforgiveness

You may not struggle with codependency. If that is you then be blessed my friend. However, you may struggle with forgiving others, harboring a grudge, or not wanting others to get off the hook so easily. Forgiveness in the scripture is the first and foremost command.

Consider these scriptures: Matt 5: 43-48 *"You have heard that it was said, 'Love your neighbor and hate your enemy.' But I tell you, love your enemies and pray for those who persecute you, that you may be children of your Father in heaven. He causes his sun to rise on the evil and the good, and sends rain on the righteous and the unrighteous. If you love those who love you, what reward will you get? Are not even the tax collectors doing that? And if you greet only your own people, what are you doing more than others? Do not even pagans do that? Be perfect, therefore, as your heavenly Father is perfect."*

Jesus is stating there that this is how God is towards you and for that person that you are so offended by. Indeed, God your father is this way towards everyone on the planet. Jesus is telling you here that you are not greater than God and therefore have no right to judge others.

Then again in the next chapter, Matt6:12 contained within the Lord's prayer we find this again *"And forgive us our debts, as we also have forgiven our debtors."* Jesus is linking your forgiveness with receiving forgiveness.

Also these scriptures: Matt 7:1-5 *"Do not judge, or you too will be judged. For in the same way you judge others, you will be judged, and with the measure you use, it will be measured to you. "Why do you look at the speck of sawdust in your brother's eye and pay no attention to the plank in your own eye? How can you say to your brother, 'Let me take the speck out of your eye,' when all the time there is a plank in your own eye? You hypocrite, first take the plank out of your own eye, and then you will see clearly to remove the speck from your brother's eye."*

Matt 18:33 *"Shouldn't you have had mercy on your fellow servant just as I had on you?"*

Luke 6:35,36 "But love your enemies, do good to them, and lend to them without expecting to get anything back. Then your reward will be great, and you will be children of the Most High, because he is kind to the ungrateful and wicked."

Ephesians 4:32 "Be kind and compassionate to one another, forgiving each other, just as in Christ God forgave you."

Forgiveness is releasing others to the care and judgment of God. Many people struggle here as they do not feel it is right to let others off the hook. There is a legalism and sense of justice that they feel in that others should be held accountable.

While this is good and understandable if you are the District Attorney or the Judge in your city or state, it is not a position that the Christian can take. To judge others is to not accurately understand your own depravity and great need for forgiveness from God Himself at all times.

Sometimes people offend us. Sometimes they mean to offend and harm us and sometimes they are ignorant of their actions. Either way we are still commissioned by Jesus and the Father, that judgment and revenge or bearing grudges is only for God the Father. Here is what Jesus said,

> **Forgiveness is releasing others to the care and judgment of God.**

John 3:17 *"For God did not send his Son into the world to condemn the world, but to save the world through him."*

Forgiveness requires humility. Jesus recognized humility as an essential requirement in walking with God and even tells us that we should follow him because of his humility. Humility to him was an outward sign of his authenticity. Matt 11:28- 30 *"Come to me, all you who are weary and burdened, and I will give you rest. Take my yoke upon you and learn from me, for I am gentle and humble in heart, and you will find rest for your souls. For my yoke is easy and my burden is light."*

1. Step one on forgiveness. Recognize you have been forgiven by God of your many eternal offenses of sin. You were lost and destined to a fiery hell of eternal separation from Him without His intervention of forgiveness through the blood of Jesus Christ your Lord. John 3:16 *"For God so loved the world that he gave his one and only Son, that whoever believes in him shall not perish but have eternal life."*

2. Stop all judging of others, here is what Jesus said, John 8:15 *"You judge by human standards; I pass judgment on no one."* Judgement freezes you in one spot and does not allow you to either give love or receive it. It isolates you and becomes a poison to your own soul.
3. Pray for those who have offended you in any way, this is the Golden Rule: Luke 6:27-36, *"But to you who are listening I say: Love your enemies, do good to those who hate you, bless those who curse you, pray for those who mistreat you." ... "Do to others as you would have them do to you." ... 35 "But love your enemies, do good to them, and lend to them without expecting to get anything back. Then your reward will be great, and you will be children of the Most High, because he is kind to the ungrateful and wicked. Be merciful, just as your Father is merciful."*

PERFECT LOVE CASTS OUT ALL FEAR

Fear is a love killer. I love how John states it. 1 John 4:18, *"There is no fear in love. But perfect love drives out fear, because fear has to do with punishment. The one who fears is not made perfect in love."*

According to John love is made complete when all fear is driven out. Think of it. How many people have you known that

> **Fear is a love killer.**

push people away that are trying to love them. If you have ever experienced that, then you recognize that when it happens the one doing the pushing away will accuse the one attempting to love them of many things. They question their motives, accusing them according to all the darkness within their own heart.

I am thinking right now of a dear friend who is now in Nicaragua as an independent missionary. She is working at making a difference. She has had to cast off a lot of fear in order to leave a wonderfully comfortable job working in her profession as a counselor. Now she is in a foreign country and even though she is of Mexican culture herself, she still is an outsider. She has meager comforts and limited support. She is following Jesus out of love.

Like anyone that is following love, there comes a point where we must choose to actively, aggressively cast off fear and embrace love. Love requires two things; vulnerability and transparency.

Vulnerability is that feeling when you're in a dream and you are standing in front of a lot of people and you realize that you are the only one without any clothes. No one else seems to notice or care, but you do. If you are like me, you will be thinking, "Where are my clothes?" Vulnerability is trusting others when it is very likely they will hurt you in some way. Then it is choosing to not be offended when they do. Further it is choosing to remain open even after they do.

Transparency is similar yet different in this way. Transparency is saying what you mean, and being honest about your thoughts, feelings, and intent. The opposite of transparency is duplicity. I think of this when I see all our presidential candidates touting how Christian they are when they are in a Christian group. One such candidate recently was espousing his Christian pedigree when he commented that he had never asked God to forgive him of anything. One might wonder why a sinless man would need a savior. I think he is being far from transparent.

But lest you think I am being too hard on him I have to tell you that I have counseled with and known many Christian leaders. They all report that they cannot be transparent with their congregations or they would face being fired or publicly persecuted by their own congregation. Most feel highly vulnerable and have strong fortified mechanisms of self-defense around them for self-protection. This too is out of fear.

But perfect love drives out all fear right. Right? This is something I face in the counseling office constantly. People come for counseling, yet put up walls and do not want to be vulnerable with a counselor. My response is that if you cannot be open and transparent here, then where? You cannot discuss these things with anyone you know, so you become an island. The trouble is that pushes everyone away and it is terribly unhealthy for you as well.

Fear has the power to isolate you from both giving and experiencing love. As we have already discussed, that is your responsibility to both give and experience. 1 John 1:7 *"But if we walk in the light, as he is in the light, we have fellowship with one another, and the blood of Jesus, his Son, purifies us from all sin."*

1 John 2:10-11 *"Anyone who loves their brother and sister lives in the light, and there is nothing in them to make them stumble. But anyone who hates a brother or sister is in the darkness and walks around in the darkness. They do not know where they are going, because the darkness has blinded them."*

Here is a quote from a popular web site 'Transparent for Christ Movement'   *"Some people's love is so superficial with so many conditions to it: I love you BECAUSE you look attractive. I love you BECAUSE you drive a nice car or have a nice house. I love you AS LONG AS you do not betray or reject me. I love you AS LONG AS you do not lie to me or steal from me. I love you UNTIL you gain weight. I love you UNTIL you lose your job. I love you IF you agree with me and take my side on everything. I love you IF you give me everything I want or feel as if I need. This is superficial love."* … *"Real love is UNRESERVED and UNCONDTIONAL. It shouldn't be preconditioned or booked in advance. Real love is unqualified—the recipient shouldn't have to say, be, or do anything to earn it. It should be extended freely. Real love is unlimited—it shouldn't run out. Real love is wholehearted—it cares about others without any thought of what it might get out of the relationship for itself. Jesus loved and served those who could do nothing for him in return except show their gratitude."* … *"Real love is VULNERABLE. It makes itself susceptible to physical or emotional attack or harm. It has no defense. It is open to be wounded. Jesus was scourged. He was beaten and whipped, but he willingly took the blows. He was mocked and blasphemed, but opened not his mouth. Jesus' love took on abuse and it didn't retaliate or try to defend itself."*x

I could not say it better myself.

Steps to Becoming More Authentic in Vulnerability and Transparency.

1. Make a commitment to be honest with yourself and others.
2. Do you hear judgmentalism, negativism, and criticism coming out of your mouth?
    a. Time for an attitude checkup.
    b. Check with someone you trust to help you with bitterness
    c. Check to see if you are angry with God.
    d. Have you been wounded by someone that should have loved you?
    e. Choose forgiveness and release that person to God, asking God to give them grace and forgiveness.
3. Are you hiding sin in your life? This is at the core of secrecy and building walls
    a. Confess sin to a confidant and someone confidential and full of grace.
4. Learn about love and healthy boundaries
    a. Practice including others
    b. Look for ways that you might be excluding others in your life, these are red flags.
5. Keep yourself sensitive to the Holy Spirit's leading and correction
    a. Allow yourself to be challenged to be more honest with others
    b. Do not take offense when others attack you for being honest
    c. Practice patience with others
    d. Forgive yourself and be graceful with yourself first then extend that to others.
6. When you find yourself acting defensively and pushing others away, choose to change
    a. Ask the Holy Spirit to give you boldness to include others.

b. Watch for anything in your life that looks like a wall instead of a fence. A fence allows other relationships; a wall separates you from others for your own protection.

LASTLY, WALK WITH THE HOLY SPIRIT.

All this love stuff is really not possible without walking in a love relationship with Father God. This is accomplished by walking with the Holy Spirit.

1 John 1:1-7 *"That which was from the beginning, which we have heard, which we have seen with our eyes, which we have looked at and our hands have touched—this we proclaim concerning the Word of life. The life appeared; we have seen it and testify to it, and we proclaim to you the eternal life, which was with the Father and has appeared to us. We proclaim to you what we have seen and heard, so that you also may have fellowship with us. And our fellowship is with the Father and with his Son, Jesus Christ. We write this to make our joy complete. This is the message we have heard from him and declare to you: God is light; in him there is no darkness at all. If we claim to have fellowship with him and yet walk in the darkness, we lie and do not live out the truth. But if we walk in the light, as he is in the light, we have fellowship with one another, and the blood of Jesus, his Son, purifies us from all sin."*

1 John 3:19-24 *"This is how we know that we belong to the truth and how we set our hearts at rest in his presence: If our hearts condemn us, we know that God is greater than our hearts, and he knows everything. Dear friends, if our hearts do not condemn us, we have confidence before God and receive from him anything we ask, because we keep his commands and do what pleases him. And this is his command: to believe in the name of his Son, Jesus Christ, and to love one another as he commanded us. The one who keeps God's commands lives in him, and he in them. And this is how we know that he lives in us: We know it by the Spirit he gave us."*

There are many scriptures in the New Testament telling us of our relationship with the Holy Spirit. I have detailed this with much discussion in other books of mine as well. Here I will list just 48 of those attributes relating to the life of the Christian and walking with the Spirit of God.

THE HOLY SPIRIT'S ROLE IN THE NEW TESTAMENT

The Spirit and the New Birth (John 3:5).
The Spirit the Well of Living Water (John 4:14).
The Spirit and True Worship (John 4:23-24).
The Spirit and the Words of Christ (John 6:63).
The Spirit and Outflowing Service (John 7:37-39).
The Spirit as the other Comforter, the Spirit of Truth (John 14:16; 15:26).
The In-breathing of the Spirit (John 20:22).
The Spirit and Power (Acts 1:8).
The -Advent of the Spirit (Acts 2:1-4).
The Outward Manifestations of the Spirit (Acts 2:1-13).
The Filling with the Spirit (Acts 4:8, 31; Eph. 5:18)
The Spirit and Ananias and Sapphira (Acts 5:3, 9).
The Holy Spirit and Obedience (Acts 5:32).
The Spirit filling Saul of Tarsus (Acts 9:17).
The Comfort of the Spirit (Acts 9:31).
The Spirit and the Gentiles (Acts 10:38-47).
Prophecy by the Spirit (Acts 11:28 and 21).
The Guidance of the Spirit (Acts 16:6, 7).
*The Holy Spirit and John's Disciples (*Acts 19:2,6)
Disobeying the Spirit of God (Acts 20:22, 23, 28; 21:4,11).
The Spirit Appointing Power in the Church (Acts 20:28)
The Spirit of Adoption and His witness to Sonship (Rom. 8:14-16).
The First-fruits of the Spirit (Rom. 8:23).
The Intercession of the Spirit (Rom. 8:26-27).
The Activities of the Spirit in the Believer (Rom. 9:1, 14:17, xv.-13, 19)
*Every Believer the Temple of the Holy Spirit (*I Cor. 3:16, 6:17).
The Baptism of the Spirit and its Scriptural Meaning (I Cor. 7:13).
The Spirit and the Gift of Tongues (1 Cor. 14:2, 14, 15, 16).
The Earnest of the Spirit (2 Cor. 1:22, 5:5; Ephes. 1:13).
The Holy Spirit in His Life-giving and Transforming Power (2 Cor. 3).
The Communion of the Holy Spirit (2 Cor. 13:14).
The Spirit Given to the Sons of God (Gal. 4:6).
Walking in the Spirit (Gal. 5:16-18).
The Fruit of the Spirit (Gal. 5:22-25).
The Spirit Sealing Every True Believer (Ephes. 1:14, 4:31).

The Access by the Spirit to the Father (Ephes. 2:18).
The Habitation of God through the Spirit (Ephes. 2:22).
The Spirit Strengthening the Inner Man (Ephes. 3:16).
The Fellowship of the Spirit (Phil. 2:1).
The Power and Assurance of the Spirit (1 Thess. 1:5-6).
The Participation in the Holy Spirit (Heb. 6:4).
The Sanctification of the Spirit (1Peter 1:2).
Obeying the Truth through the Spirit (1 Peter 1:22)
The Unction of the Spirit (I John 2:20-27).
Knowing the Truth by the Spirit (I John 2:27).
Christ Abiding in the Believer by the Spirit (I John 3:24, 8:13).
The Realizing Power of the Spirit (1 John 5:6-8).
Praying in the Spirit (Jude, verse 20).
The Holy Spirit in His Own Completeness (Rev. 1:4, 3:1, 4:5).
The Longing of the Spirit (Rev. 21:17).[xi]

THE IMPORTANT ROLE OF BELIEF

The longer I live the more I realize the importance of belief. I have always taught my patients, groups, clients, and fellow Christians that there are two things that motivate any and everything you do; believe and need.

If I believe that the freeway will be backed up and I need to get to work as quickly as possible I will take an alternate route, even though it may take me about 10 minutes longer. On a personal level, I dealt with many in the hospital that have a difficult time believing that anyone could love them. So, they do not love themselves, at least not very easily. Consequently, they do not accept loving acts or words from others easily. In fact, they will tend to demean or degrade any act, or thought, or words of love and affection. They tend to dumb it down a bit, if not dismiss it altogether.

For a husband to tell his wife, "You are beautiful" is easy, right? But what if she is 80? What if she is overweight by 50 pounds? Then she might be more likely to respond, "Yea right!" But what if he really means it? What if he feels it from his heart? Her dismissal may come as a hurtful thing. Her response may sound something like, "I know what you want!"

I have to say, from me to you, I have struggled with allowing myself to be loved by others. There has been something kind of broken on the inside for most of my life. When working with my patients I began to see the extremes of what I have struggled with for so long.

Here it is in a nutshell then. Your ability to experience love from God is a direct reflection of your belief about how valuable you are to Him. This ability to experience love from God, affects every living relationship you have. This is why belief in the scripture is so very important.

> **Your ability to experience love from God is a direct reflection of your belief about how valuable you are to Him.**

I looked at this in some detail in my book ***The God Partnership: A Spiritual Awakening,*** *"For many, if not most in the church, there exists this fundamental belief that we are basically evil inside and out as individuals. It is profound in that this belief affects absolutely everything you will do in your life. It will affect every relationship and every task. If you believe you are fundamentally evil then you will also believe that you do not deserve love, you do not deserve blessings, and you do not have any basic right to ask or expect any of these things in your life from God or anyone else. This is why we hear so many people praying, "Jesus if it is your will that my loved one not die of cancer, then please, I beg of you, please have mercy on her/him and heal them." With this attitude we feel as though we have to beg God that somehow we love people much more than He does and we have to change His mind away from just letting us die in our sickness."*[xii]

In the God Partnership book I ask the question relating to God, **"How are you responding to God? Your perspective will determine your experience and will limit it greatly."** Ultimately your perspective is a direct reflection of your belief. Belief is the great dividing point of what happens in the Christian life and what does not happen.

The same is true of our relationships. If you believe that your mate doesn't love you, then you will discount everything they do for you. The same is true of any relationship. Especially with those of authority. When your belief that no one loves you is strong enough, it will even destroy the relationship mothers have with their children.

I have watched hundreds of women that have been abused from childhood find it impossible to receive or believe that their own children love them. When meeting with the families they will often report that it is impossible to make their mom happy. They will likely never go on vacation, and live a life they feel is in constant service to others. Yet as for receiving love and affection, it is little and far in between.

This of course becomes a real sticking point in love. If any of this sounds the least bit familiar in your own experience or something you experience with others, then you know what I am talking about here.

Most people either see God as being distant and uncaring or a hard exacting taskmaster that is quite frankly weary of people in our sinful mess. We're like Adam in the garden when God came like normal and then began to call for him. Who changed? Adam changed! Not just his sin, but Adam changed his very belief system about God as a person. That disconnect created within all of us a predisposition of unbelief, suspicion, fear, guilt, and shame, all from our own inner conflict created from choosing darkness over light.

When Adam and Eve changed within the Garden of Eden, they changed perspective for all human kind that would follow. We have a natural prejudice towards receiving and believing that God is loving, kind, and benevolent towards us.

I believe this is the death Father God was talking about, that on that day when you eat of the tree of the knowledge of good and evil you will surely die. Genesis 2: 15-17 *"The Lord God took the man and put him in the Garden of Eden to work it and take care of it. And the Lord God commanded the man, "You are free to eat from any tree in the garden; but you must not eat from the tree of the knowledge of good and evil, for when you eat from it you will certainly die."*

What died in us was this natural ability to love and be loved. It has been a battlefield for mankind from that day forward. Suspicion, fear, hurt, offense, resentment, bitterness, unforgiveness, resentment, envy, strife and many other descriptors all point us to this beginning.

Thank God for Jesus, the only begotten of the Father. Through his great sacrifice you have been giving a new life and freedom through the eternal life in the Holy Spirit. Remember, you have been created in God's very image. Since you are born again by the Spirit of God, you become a new creation. You pass from darkness to light, from death to life, from old to new. You are now a kingdom of priests, and no longer a captive to bondage. It is for freedom that you have been set free. As Paul states in his Gospel, Galatians 5:1 *"It is for freedom that Christ has set us free. Stand firm, then, and do not let yourselves be burdened again by a yoke of slavery."*

Belief is the most critical thing we do all day. The beginning point of getting free to love is to aggressively confront our natural tendency to discount love. It is easy to quote 1 Corinthians 13.

Love is patient and kind,

Love **does not** envy or boast, or take delight in anything evil- but rejoices with the truth (transparency and integrity),

Love **is not** proud, rude, self-seeking, or easily angered,

Love **always** protects, trusts, hopes, perseveres

Love never fails

There are three that remain, Faith, Hope, and Love

And the greatest of these is Love.

If you aggressively confront your own heart and mind daily with this reality of what Love is, you will transform your experience of giving and receiving real love.

The mind is your battlefield. You need to transform this old belief system that God does not really love you and others cannot truly or fully love me either. You receive transformation by washing your heart, mind, and spirit with God's Truth.

John 8:32 *"Then you will know the truth, and the truth will set you free."*

John 1:14 *"The Word became flesh and made his dwelling among us. We have seen his glory, the glory of the one and only Son, who came from the Father, full of grace and truth."*

John 1:17 *"For the law was given through Moses; grace and truth came through Jesus Christ."*

John 8:36 *"So if the Son sets you free, you will be free indeed."*

Romans 6:18 *"You have been set free from sin and have become slaves to righteousness."*

Romans 6:22 *"But now that you have been set free from sin and have become slaves of God, the benefit you reap leads to holiness, and the result is eternal life."*

Romans 8:2 *"because through Christ Jesus the law of the Spirit who gives life has set you free from the law of sin and death."*

1 Corinthians 7:22 *"For the one who was a slave when called to faith in the Lord is the Lord's freed person; similarly, the one who was free when called is Christ's slave."*

2 Corinthians 3:17 *"Now the Lord is the Spirit, and where the Spirit of the Lord is, there is freedom."*

8 Steps to Walking With God

1. Give your heart, mind, body, and soul to God.
2. Make a conscious choice to turn toward God.
3. Ask God to reveal Himself to you.
4. Confess your sin to God, and receive the work of the death, burial, and resurrection of Jesus. Accept that His eternal blood paid once and for all time the price of your own sin.
5. Choose to walk forward with a learning spirit to connect with God's people wherever God leads you, and learn the Bible and its whole message.
6. Choose to implement all that you learn. Ask for God's help to change those things about yourself that need changing along that journey.
7. Keep on keeping on in that refining process as you allow the Father to speak to you through His Holy Spirit.
8. God is light and God is love, choose light and choose love everywhere you find it.

Questions to Ponder:

Challenging your inner prejudice of unbelief

Be honest with yourself here. Are you giving others in your life full credit for all their loving acts of kindness towards you?

List 5 ways you can show appreciation for that love, to each person (you should need a sheet of paper here)

When will you act on those things listed?

Can you identify ways in which you find yourself holding back in love towards God?

Are there things you are hiding from God? List them here.

Invite God into that space with you and ask God to empower your belief in His ability to help you fulfill your needs, desires, hopes, and dreams.

Invite God into your deepest inmost self and ask him to both heal you in love and set you free to love.

Find time to commune with God.

List all the things God has done to bless you. Start with the air you are breathing and the life you are living.

Love and the Partnership Principle

If I shift in my understanding that God loves me for who I am and not for what I can do, it changes the very motivation of why I come to Him, and especially why He comes to me. In my book *"**The God Partnership: A Spiritual Awakening**"* I explore this in more detail. To make it as brief as possible here I will define it as this: <u>God loves you for who you are.</u> Do not forget, God created you and knit you together in the womb. He has already put inside of you part of His own character and image. He has given you His Holy Spirit that is working to transform you, starting in your spirit, bringing it to a new birth and bringing it into life. Then His spirit is now and has always been working on your heart to transform it into the perfect image of God. There is far more God there than you can imagine and you can tap into that at any moment.

> Love comes from God and the love that comes out of you is an expression of the very residency of God Himself in you.

Second, God has been working in you so that you can begin to trust in what He is building and revealing within your own heart. He is working to bring you into wholeness of self - body, mind, heart, and spirit. The more whole you become the more freedom you experience. The more freedom you experience then the more love you are able to receive and give at the same time. Love comes from God and the love that comes out of you is an expression of the very residency of God Himself in you.

As I have said before in my books, **<u>the opposite of love is use, manipulation, domination, and control.</u>** These four James calls selfish ambition - concern only for the self and self-gratification. In this mindset, others are expected to be subservient, to submit, and to cow-tow to the demands of the one in charge. This not only is <u>not love</u>, it <u>is not God.</u> God does not lead this way.

Surely God is always in charge, but God never dominates your will. He always leads you by invitation into wholeness, fullness, and wellbeing. God wants you to discover yourself fully and to find the ultimate freedom of the expression of your destiny by allowing Him to empower you in your journey. You cannot complete your journey and destiny without Him. He has designed you and your destiny to be complete in a partnership with Himself, doing things for you that you cannot do for or by yourself. The idea of a self-made man is completely ridiculous as no one has created himself and created the world or the cosmos, much less created the very womb that would give him birth. How self-absorbed such thinking is. Indeed, thousands of others had tremendous input into me becoming me. I did not create myself.

Any love relationship is a partnership. All love relationships you experience will be directly affected and a reflection of your perceived love relationship with Father God. View Him as demanding and exacting or judgmental, then all your other relationships will be colored with that mentality. View Him as benevolent, forgiving and full of grace and that will color all your relationships with that grace. See Him as constantly working on your behalf to cause you to succeed and you will find yourself working diligently to cause the success in all others around you. It is an inescapable principle of reciprocity.

GETTING YOUR WAY: THE MAGIC BALANCE OF DOING GOOD FOR OTHERS AND MYSELF.

Why is it important to get your way? We have already seen that even Jesus worked to get his way. He did so while never betraying his own will or his own way. He also did so without ever taking away the freedom of choice of others to find their own will or way.

Let's take a close look at the subtlety of this dynamic. John 21:17, ***"The third time he said to him, "Simon son of John, do you love me?"***

Peter was hurt because Jesus asked him the third time, "Do you love me?" He said, "Lord, you know all things; you know that I love you." Jesus said, "Feed my sheep."

Here Jesus has come to the disciples who had gone fishing. They had gone back to what they knew. In essence Peter had led the other disciples to get back to work at their old vocations. In the verses just before this scene, they had been fishing all night, when someone on the shore shouted out to them asking them if they had caught anything. They had not. He shouted to cast their nets on to the other side of the boat. They were a bit put off at the arrogance of the one on the shore, yet something familiar about that voice carried over the waters. They could barely hear just over 100 yards away with the sound of the water slapping against the side of the little boat. They cast their nets out and caught a large amount of fish. John, Jesus' half-brother said it is the Lord, and Peter immediately swam to shore. Jesus already had a fire with some fish of his own and bread. This is the setting.

Remember just days before was the crucifixion where Peter had denied Jesus three times the night before. Here Jesus affirms Peter's love three times. Peter needed that and didn't realize it. But there is more. Jesus is actually inviting Peter into a completely new life. Peter is familiar with this new life in some ways as he has been following Jesus for 3 years. But now Jesus is asking Peter to finally, once for all buy a ticket, get on the train and never look back.

"Then feed my sheep." It is a full time job and the Father will take care of his every need. To take this new mantle Peter will have to leave his old job behind. He will have to leave his old way of making a living and defining his manhood behind. Peter is remembering Jesus' first invitation to him when he was fishing with his brother Andrew, "I will make you fishers of men." Matt 4:*19 "And He said to them, "Follow Me, and I will make you fishers of men "Immediately they left their nets and followed Him...."*

Everything has led to this moment in time for Peter. Peter has a choice. Continue as a fisherman struggling on his own all through the day and night to catch a few fish, or to listen to Jesus' voice and follow him and <u>become a fisher of men</u> and feed the children of God.

Jesus is not taking over Peter's life. Jesus is opening a door for Peter's destiny. However, it will take an agreement from Peter to walk through that door and step into his destiny.

What does this have to do with Love? This is at the very core of love. Love leads by invitation. Love calls someone into their destiny. Love never settles for comfort or a place of compromise. Love does not ask what are you most comfortable with, rather it is much more likely to challenge comfort and inspire one to stretch themselves into becoming someone greater, moving closer to authentic love, truth, and enlightenment. Love does not condemn. Love does not capitulate, cajole, does not intimidate. Love does challenge others and self to move forward. Love does not manipulate for selfish gain, gratification, or advantage. Love always invites.

Will Peter advance the kingdom of God? Most certainly! But he will do so always at the strengthening of his own self and fulfillment of all the purposes already built within his own heart. Peter will free himself from the fish nets and will learn to walk the way of the salvation net. For him it made all the difference.

Peter will experience the incredible, powerful love of God and will demonstrate that to the world for the rest of his life. He will build the first church that will transform the world. All because love called him out of himself into true freedom of self.

Let's look again at 2 Peter 1:3-11 where Peter links love with choice. He lists kindness, goodness, and love as something each person bears a personal responsibility to achieve, experience, maintain, and demonstrate outwardly, as well as feel inwardly (regardless of how others are treating you). Peter has a lifetime of experience being this first Apostle-Evangelist-Pastor when he writes this in 2 Peter 1:3-9

3: His divine power has given us everything we need for life and godliness

<u>Through</u> our <u>True</u> <u>Knowledge</u> (epignosis) of Him who called us by his own glory and goodness.

<u>Through these</u> he has given us his very great and precious promises, so that

<u>Through them</u> you may participate in the divine nature and escape the corruption in the world caused by evil desires.

5 For this very reason, make every effort to ADD to your faith:

Virtue /goodness (arête) and to goodness,

Knowledge (gnosis) and to knowledge,

Self-Control; and to self-control,

Perseverance; and to perseverance,

Godliness; and to godliness, brotherly

Kindness; and to brotherly kindness,

Love.

8 For if you possess these qualities in increasing measure, they will keep you from being ineffective and unproductive in your knowledge of our Lord Jesus Christ. But if anyone does not have them, he is nearsighted and blind, and has forgotten that he has been cleansed from his past sins.

So we see here that my experience of love is not bound up in how others are treating me. Love springs forth from that επιγνοσισ, epignosis, the true experiential knowledge with the Living God. It moves beyond knowing about love, to experiencing a love relationship. Then out of that flows access to the divine, access to receive all the promises of God, and the freedom over all our fleshliness.

Peter teaches us that out of my relationship with God, it is now my responsibility to be diligent in the pursuit of those seven qualities, virtuously choosing, knowledge to know with the intellect, apply what I learn from God with diligence, and keep on applying. Then I will begin to experience a type of goodness in my life that will lead to expressing kindness to others and myself. Finally I will experience the giving and receiving of authentic love.

> **Love springs forth from your true experiential knowledge of the Living God.**

PASSIVE AGGRESSIVE: THE UNHEALTHY SIDE OF LOVE

When discussing love we must look at the often subtle differences of what we call passive aggressive behaviors and codependent behaviors. I will look at each from the point of view of caretaker vs. caregiver.

Passive aggressive is any behavior that seeks to control in a way that is indirect, attempting to hide one's intent or motive. It is subversive in nature. It is my distinct belief that authentic love is transparent. It leads by an open invitation with transparent motivations. This kind of love can and will often be misunderstood and misrepresented by those whose hearts have been trapped by fear, anger, unforgiveness, and the mistrust of others.

"Murphy and Oberlin also see passive aggression as part of a larger umbrella of hidden anger stemming from ten traits of the angry child or adult. These traits include making one's own misery, the inability to analyze problems, blaming others, turning bad feelings into angry ones, attacking people, lacking empathy, using anger to gain power, confusing anger with self-esteem, and indulging in negative self-talk. Lastly, the authors point out that those who hide their anger can be nice when they wish to be.[xiii]

Another definition: "passive-aggressive behavior is characterized by a habitual pattern of passive resistance to expected work requirements, opposition, stubbornness, and negative attitudes in response to requirements for normal performance levels expected of others. Most frequently it occurs in the workplace where resistance is exhibited by such indirect behaviors as procrastination, <u>forgetfulness</u>, and purposeful inefficiency, especially in reaction to demands by <u>authority figures</u>,[xiv]

The term 'passive aggressive' is often used to describe women in many situations, yet men can be as much and perhaps even more so. In the literature, people describe passive aggressive behavior as anything ranging from simple tardiness to highly manipulative back stabbing behavior rooted in deep-seated anger, distain, and even outright hatred.

I certainly think these responses are possible. For our purposes here, I wish to keep a focus on passive aggressive behavior within the perspective of how one gets their way, especially in relation to the love relationship. I tend to think those writing the above descriptions have a particularly negative interpretation of passive aggressive behavior. I believe there is something lacking in those definitions. Let's face it, the passive aggressive way of getting one's way is a learned behavior largely thrust upon one by fate. Yes I said fate. It is a learned behavior not because one has a defect of some kind, but rather due to simple factors like birth order or the family system one is born into.

I often find that the youngest among siblings will tend to be the passive aggressive one in the pack. It is a matter of survival and learning to get one's way amongst all the older family members. They simply take what they want. If one has a brother that outweighs him four to one sitting on his chest, it's a matter of survival to a six year old.

But there are many circumstances where one's ability to simply ask for what they need and receive it, can be taken away. One may have parents or siblings with emotional disorders or needs that weigh upon the child in some way. He or she feels guilty or threatened if they express, need, want, desire, unhappiness, anger, frustration, or any emotion that elicits a response from the adult or older family members which they are unprepared to address. The statement "stop crying or I will give you something to cry about" comes to mind.

Children of alcoholic or substance abusing parents is another situation that is common. When you have to care for a drunken parent that is smashing things and hitting people, one learns passive aggressive means to survive. In today's society when we have gone completely into accepting the idea of people smoking marijuana daily, I am afraid we are breeding an entire generation of passive aggressive, struggling people. Our lax mentality of accepting "recreational" drug usages of all kinds is on the rise. As a health care professional I have personally spoken to thousands of families with such abuses taking place. I have treated the addicted parents, and dealt with the broken children and the children's children. Recreational substance abuse has a tremendous cost on the family extending for generations.

> **Just like it is not healthy for someone to get their way all the time, it's not healthy for someone to never get their way.**

I tend to have a lot of compassion for the family. If you are in any situation like that, I strongly encourage you to seek help. Start reading about boundaries. Google it and start reading. Read Caretaking verses Caregiving. Get in a free boundaries class at a church. Start a journey to your own recovery.

Let's face it, everyone needs to get their way at some point. Our world exists with these dynamics at play everywhere you go. From the grocery store, movie theater, doctors office, on the job and even at (or especially at) church. There are more aggressive and lesser aggressive people and it is just fine to be either. Just like it is not healthy for someone to get their way all the time, it's not healthy for someone to never get their way.

Someone getting their way all the time can lead to one that is either spoiled or a complete tyrant. On the other hand people never getting their way tends to lead to a revolt at some point. For many passive aggressive types that have extreme difficulty asking for what they need, they eventually find that living alone is the most peaceful existence possible.

Being with someone can be a full time job attending to their needs. It is just easier to live alone. The tension comes into play as most passive aggressive types need someone to care for and they feel quite alone without that. That is where the unhealthy part begins to act like a corrosive on the metal of the relationship, slowly eating away at authentic love.

The most extreme forms of passive aggressive behavior results when one cannot receive love or acts of love without accusing the one showing the love of ulterior motives. They accuse them of really being selfish and trying to manipulate with good deeds. Of course this is a direct form of projection, where they are actually projecting their own motives onto the actions of others. Most relationships suffering from this end poorly.

Examples would be the husband that is cheating on his wife or submerged in porn, then accusing her of being disloyal or unfaithful. The wife that accuses the husband of being selfish while she secretly spends all the extra cash on clothes and jewelry. She will have hundreds of pairs of shoes and he only a few. Or the wife accusing the husband of being selfish and not really caring while he is rubbing her back, helping with housework and caring for the children, all while working multiple jobs. Then she will deny him sex as he really is so selfish and doesn't really love her. Another case I have heard quite frequently is when the husband does not work, stays at home, sometimes he cares for a child, sometimes not. The wife is the bread winner yet he constantly degrades her and demeans her, and even accuses her of being unfaithful. Later she finds out that he has been sleeping around on her.

The passive aggressive behavior becomes a constant stream of confessions of what is actually bound up in their own heart. Every accusation becomes a telltale sign of an actual confession and revelation of how they feel about themselves secretly. The inner conflict will bring any relationship to a point of no return if not dealt with.

If you do not suffer from any of these maladies, count your lucky stars. Yet this section will definitely help you shed light on others that you know and the dynamics that are at play with them. This section will also help you understand the lady at work that tends to overreact when given extra tasks, or the guy that acts like he runs the place. In either case, someone has given too much power or taken away too much power from someone.

You might be asking, "Why on earth does this matter?" Good question! It is perhaps the single most important question that most couples face. I have rarely seen a family system where there was not one or more members of the family dealing with having to be passive aggressive in order to get their way, at least a little of the time.

If there is difficulty in asking for what one wants, needs, or desires then tension will begin. That tension eventually leads to anger, resentment, bitterness, accusations, unforgiveness, and then entitlements. Entitlements subvert any love relationship.

Entitlements are actually little contracts and compromises we make with ourselves. It goes something like this: My wife doesn't really love me so I am justified in seeking love elsewhere. My husband doesn't love me so I am justified in spending a lot of money on myself, or flirting with the man that is showing me so much attention at work.

I do not wish to go too deep here but I will say that such entitlements are usually rooted in beliefs about one's own self that stems from childhood rejections, neglect, abuses, and lack of healthy positive nurturing parents and siblings. These beliefs naturally carry over into adult love relationships. You simply cannot become another person with a totally different world view just because you say "I DO." In fact the opposite becomes true. You actually give each other permission to be your most natural self, and so these beliefs surface quite rapidly.

The bottom line is that we all need to be able to ask for what we need, want, and desire. We all need to be able to freely express our thoughts, feelings, and concerns. This is the goal and nature of Authentic Love. It leads by invitation, not threats and accusations. Love always acts in the best interest of the other person while at the same time preserving one's own best interest.

For the passive aggressive there is a constant struggle to find the right way to ask for what they want, need, desire, or to express honestly the feelings or thoughts they are experiencing. So it becomes problematic in how life is lived out on a daily basis. It may continue until the kids are raised, then everything changes, and with just the two of you, it is like the proverbial elephant in the living room.

Here is a typical passive aggressive situation. To be honest this could either be male or female to be fair. However it is 3 times as likely to be female.

Mary is a hard working mother of 3 boys and devoted wife. She never directly asks for much and is always picking up after everyone. Mary's husband likes this arrangement very much as he is never challenged about spending money on his truck, his hunting trips or fishing gear. Mary is getting weary though. She is constantly asking her husband for help with the children and to do chores around the house. Her husband is oblivious, and calls her a nag and a martyr.

Mary asks for a Saturday to go do things with her sister. She needs her husband to keep the boys and do something with them for the day. She asks like this: "My sister is going to a women's conference and she has asked me to go. I told her that I would have to ask you and that I might consider it if you wanted me to go."

Of course does the husband 'want' his wife to go? Not in a million years. He is thinking —"women's conference, sounds horrible, a bunch of women getting all kinds of funny ideas about women's liberation. He responds with some disparaging remarks and then capitulates to her after significantly displaying his repulsion at the idea.

"Do you want to go to something like that? It sounds so boring." She responds, "Well it was just an idea."

"Fine, all settled then. Just tell her no." He has no clue what a deep hole he has just dug for himself!

Of course the truly passive aggressive type here gets hurt and offended at the first disparaging remark coming out of his mouth, that look on his face, and his distain. What he so often does not realize is that she has a growing hurt in her that is turning into bitterness and is adding to a wounded spirit from childhood. He will one day likely leave her for another woman as her inner anger and inner disrespect for him grows. She will unwittingly display that in a million different ways non-verbally to him and he will feel empowered to seek approval from another woman more understanding of him. She will be justified in all her blame and hatred of such a pig.

He on the other hand will be telling his new wife, "I could never do anything to make her happy. No matter what I ever did, it was wrong. It was never enough. She made me feel guilty for everything."

About a third of you reading this will undoubtedly be stinging right about now. Some of these things will be ringing true of you or someone you know.

I have seen and treated well over a thousand of these men and women as inpatients in the hospital and in private practice over the years. Their self-image is similar to their picture of Jesus as all loving and all caring yet never demanding. They always have a picture of Jesus as never expecting love in return. They feel that if you simply ask for what you want and what you need directly, and do not accept no for an answer, then that is selfish and not loving.

In the view of the passive aggressive mind, those who go through life expecting to get what they want are unloving and uncaring ultimately, and yet they are constantly drawn to those who know what they want. Of course when they want 'You', then of course they are the greatest person on the planet. This becomes a vicious cycle of attraction and blame shifting. They are trapped in a maze of never coming to a resolution of what to do to meet each other's needs, wants, or desires.

In the end no one is happy, because even when asked directly, the passive aggressive person cannot directly state what they want. This is a matter of a belief that goes to their core. They do not believe that they have the same rights and privileges as everyone else. The way they know life is that others will use them. It's inevitable and there is nothing anyone can do to change that.

Somewhere in their childhood that right to ask directly for what they want, need, or desire has been stripped from them, and the demand to care for others who should be caring for themselves was placed upon them. They most likely have no clue what is going on. Their observation is that they cannot pick a good mate. They are always getting taken advantage of by husbands, children, brothers, sisters, and especially anyone in authority.

Of course it should be sufficient to say that happiness comes from a combination of the pursuit of meaning, balanced and fulfilling lifelong relationships, and diligently hanging onto an attitude with a positive determination. "Having meaning in one's life is positively linked to well-being and happiness, and negatively linked to depression (Steger, Frazier, Oishi, & Kaler, 2006; Steger et al., 2009)."[xv]

What makes this an important facet of love? You might even ask what this has to do with a loving relationship at all. Some people seem to view love as though it is a state that you have no control over whatsoever. They believe that you simple fall into love. Their partners are also the first ones coming into the office declaring, "My partner does not love me anymore. They have found someone else." Of course, if it is a lady telling me this, her husband has found someone younger and more beautiful and sexually active. If it is a man telling me this, his wife has fallen in love with someone such as her boss or some fellow that is more emotionally and financially secure.

> **The reality is that love is chosen.**

The reality is that love is chosen. Chemistry has to be there for sure, yet anyone that has lived very long can assure you that chemistry changes constantly. Moods, emotions, hormones, brain and body chemistry, all fluctuate. Of course as a mental health professional this is my field, helping people find a balance in all the fluctuations of life. Brain and body chemistry are just two components of that picture and I can assure you they are very real. You might be amazed at how much power and control you have over directing those thoughts, feelings, and brain-body chemistry. As we have said earlier, you can change your brain chemistry in just 6 seconds with a 6 second hand shake or hug.

After falling in love, many people may begin taking on offences. Others just begin considering their options. In today's world we have adopted a mindset that cohabitation is best. Somehow we think that living together in a trial period is a great idea. I have talked with many people from all walks of life who were trying it on for a while to see if it is a good fit. This is really a cover-up for their real motivation.

I have talked with many couples who cohabitated for 4, 6, 8, 13, and 17 years even. Then they get married and within two years are getting a divorce. People are always surprised and baffled by this.

The reason is that marriage means something. That is why they waited so long to tie the knot. If marriage meant nothing, then either no one would get married or everyone would get married; either way it would never be an issue.

Studies actually show that people who cohabitate are really waiting for something better to come along. This just makes it more legitimate in their own mind. For the one doing the leaving, they think it might be just fine. For the one being left after eight years and two children later, as you can imagine they are the one calling me. It is not so fine for them. The idea of keeping all your options open so that you might find something better might sound good, but is just does not pan out so practically or statistically.

It simply falls under the category of "use, manipulation, domination, and control." In the end when one is done "using" another person, they discard them like a worn out shirt. To be sure, both partners had to agree to the "using" of each other, but that legitimizes nothing. This is not only crushing to any adult, it is devastating to a daughter or a son. You cannot imagine how many adults I have sat and talked with that told the story of their parent who left them to go off and start another family, thereby excluding them.

Authentic love seeks to always be transparent and inclusive. Authentic love will always seek the very best for the other person while not excluding one's own self from the equation. Real love always includes respect and love for one's own self. Authentic love does not assume responsibility for another person's actions, thoughts, feelings, moods, emotions, duties, or things that one can and must do for themselves. To do that is rescuing and becoming a caretaker and stops being a caregiver.

I am reminded of a comment my wife used to make to our granddaughters when they would cry or hurt themselves in some way. "You poor little thing!" The trouble with this comment is that it makes a declaration that the one you are wanting to rescue is first poor, then little or smaller than the problem or feeling that they are experiencing, and finally a thing. It also is also declaring this person is defined in such a way. Of course a poor thing has to be rescued by a more powerful person. Don't get me wrong here. I am so glad my wife has the heart of a real grandmother and the thought can be endearing. So we have learned more positive ways of endearing ourselves to our grandchildren, like "Oh you beautiful, sweet, bright little girl."

You might say I am being too picky here. I don't think so though. If I am constantly saying things that take someone's power away from them even in small ways then I am training that person to be dependent upon me. I will also be telling them that they do not have power in many small ways which eventually leads to disempowerment in many larger ways. Eventually everyone gets stuck and the loving relationship unravels and falls apart.

In the realm of the church and personal growth as a Christian, the focus of our love is to empower people to become everything they are destined to be. In the realm of the psychological, we are constantly working to move people in the direction of empowerment to achieve, overcome, and achieve their fullest potential.

When I assume responsibility for someone else, then I am taking away the power they should have in their own life. Though many relationships start this way and people feel "cared for" as they have never been cared for in their life, it can lead to domination and control if it gets out of hand. It can happen by either partner, the one doing the care taking or the one being cared for.

Many men start this way in relationships being this doting, very attentive and caring romantic man. Occasionally this wonderful man will begin to morph after marriage. He will work to get the wife more and more isolated and estranged from her other relationships to be exclusively with him. He will then work to isolate her from friends and family and even distance them in proximity from others so that they can have all this time together. Eventually he becomes more and more critical and then condemning and threatening, all the time brutalizing her emotionally and perhaps even physically.

TED Talks has a great talk given about such a relationship by Leslie Morgan. I recommend this talk to all my female patients dealing with spousal abuse. By the way, a number of husbands find themselves in this situation. Men are far less likely to make a change and break out of such a relationship as they generally are not being physically threatened. Further they have a male pride that is like an iron gate that does not let them embrace the truth. They are in a cage. The key to escape is on a string around their own neck so to speak. They refuse to believe anyone telling them they have the key. Feel it, break the string, take the key and unlock the gate, and go free.

The other side of this control is when the wife most often, (but sometimes the man), dotes over her mate and family. They serve them and seem to have a need to please. They wait hand and foot, year after year on everyone. They seldom if ever ask for anything for themselves. Where to eat dinner and vacation spots are all decided by everyone else, as is the money spent on everyone else's clothes and hobbies.

I tend to see these women in the hospital inpatient environment with suicidal attempts when their children hit their twenties. The story goes something like this: "I have done everything for everyone else and everyone hates me." The truth of the situation is that everyone is wanting to have freedom to live their own lives in their own direction.

The complaint of everyone else is twofold. First they see her as controlling everything. Second is that no one can do anything to please her. Why? She has no life. She has made her life living through them. She has thrived on gaining her only source of self-esteem on being needed by them. Now that they have minds and feelings of their own, they want to live life in their own direction. She cannot let go as she has no life of her own. When she realizes this is when depression and desperation sets in. She will be face to face with the reality of those childhood issues which she never dealt with of not feeling loved or having never experienced authentic love. And she certainly is not experiencing it now.

Questions to Consider:

Let's be honest here, do you give in some relationships in order to get something in return?

Have you ever felt offended in a relationship and ended it badly?

Do you judge people quickly?

Do you tend to write people off?

Do you find it easy to forgive others and look the other way?

Name 5 people you forgave of major offenses in the past 10 years.

Do you still have relationship with any of these?

Is there anything you feel Jesus might do differently in your situation?

Flip side: Has anyone ever described you as insensitive or uncaring?

Do you have past relationships that you have used or taken advantage of others?

Name 5 ways you could have been more loving in those relationships.

The Rational Case for Love

I find myself in the midst of a generation that is bent on expressing every form of Godless behavior and character that we can imagine. We have cast off all moral constraints within marriage and love relationships. Love has been replaced by lust and our society doesn't seem to be aware.

In my work as a counselor I have worked with a number of single Christian women. Nearly all of them have revealed to me that when a relationship gets even the least bit serious, the men want to have sex before they do anything else. It is a requirement to which they – the men, feel entitled. These are Christian men I am talking about. Think about that for a moment. These men may even be in leadership positions that you respect.

Of course not all pastors and Christian leaders are immoral. Yet it is as common as not to see Christian people living in cohabitation rather than marriage, and just as common to know most of your friends are in their second or third marriage.

> **Love is about rules that govern relationships**

If the marriage relationship suffers this reality, then so too do all other relationships suffer.

Love is about rules that govern relationships. The love rules as outlined in this book have been the standard around which our western civilization has been built for the past 1700 years. Though our western culture has not always abided by those rules, we have grown increasingly stronger in them. Those rules have become more clearly defined throughout the centuries.

The attempts to dismantle those love rules in our courts of law, governmental bodies, schools, universities, military, and industrial settings have been moving at a rapid pace.

Yet in all this "progress" regarding liberties in our society, as a counselor I do not see progress by individuals or families. I see people engaging in freedoms that follow the four words of selfish ambition fully at work; **USE, MANIPULATION, DOMINATION, AND CONTROL.**

When we see someone dominating and acting as a dictator, ignoring the will of the people and imposing his personal will over millions who have expressed their will and desire differently, then this is not love. It is manipulation, domination, and control.

It is true on a personal level as well. The woman coming in for counseling whose husband is emotionally, verbally, and even physically abusive, describes this same mentality. He is domineering, controlling, putting her down, and subjugating her to his will. It is easily defined as use, manipulation, domination, and control. This is again the opposite of love and what we consider common, courteous, mutual respect and concern for another.

With everyone out for their own agenda, the number seeking the common good is getting weaker and weaker, resulting in the rise of people in distress and crisis. Those who will sacrifice for the greater good are generally viewed as useful fodder for the ambitious, to use for their own advancement or agenda. How do I know this? Because when such servants actually need anything in return, they are quickly dismissed and tossed aside, and are likely to be branded as disloyal.

But you can choose to be different. You can choose to change the direction of your life and thereby change your destiny. When you change your destiny, you change the destiny of the generations that follow you.

Matthieu Ricard of the Mind and Life Institute has written extensively about this case for changing the world by simple acts of change within your own life. In his latest book ***Altruism: The Power of Compassion to Change Yourself and the World,*** Ricard defines altruism is the benevolent act of kindness to another in order to alleviate their pain or suffering in some way.

He makes an extensive case for selfish self-centeredness as being by nature the opposite of authentic love, and a disregard for the plight of others in order to maintain one's own comfort level. Ricard offers many studies that show how altruism, which I call here acts of love, benefits not only the person being ministered to but also the one doing the giving. We have already seen this demonstrated in the prior chapters.

Ricard goes on to link selfishness and self-centerless with the Buddhist's perspective of being one of the things that poisons mankind. He states, *"Many of our sufferings are rooted in hatred, greed, selfishness, pride, jealousy, and other mental states that Buddhism groups under the term "mental poisons" because they literally poison our and others' existences."*

> **You do not have to be a Christian to recognize that authentic love benefits mankind as well as transforms the soul.**

Love or altruism is then the opposite of these poisons. Altruism is a powerful force that has the ability to change us from the inside out. *"The pursuit of a selfish happiness is doomed to failure, whereas accomplishing the good of others constitutes one of the main factors for fulfillment and, ultimately, progress toward Enlightenment."*... xvi As Shantideva, a seventh-century Indian Buddhist master, writes in his work, The Path Towards Awakening: All the joy the world contains has come through wishing happiness for others. All the misery the world contains has come through wanting pleasure for oneself. Is there need for lengthy explanation? Childish beings look out for themselves; Buddha's labor for the good of others: See the difference that divides them!"xvii

You do not have to be a Christian to recognize that authentic love benefits mankind as well as transforms the soul. Ricard proves this is a naturally occurring force within all mankind and it has the power to change and transform self and society.

He quotes many studies on rats, moles, bats, and many people groups. These studies link the levels of Oxytocin to maternal love further demonstrate how benevolent social behavior increases these chemicals. With their increase there is a corresponding increase in the capacity to show and receive affection and empathy towards others as well as increase stability, confidence and calmness in the individual. He demonstrates the connection between altruistic actions and individual and social benefit.

One thing I appreciate about Ricard's book is his devotion to the subject. He gives illustrated story after story of altruism, 'Love' in people's real lives. Here are two such stories.

"During World War II, Irene Gut Opdyke risked her life many times to save Jews threatened with death in Poland. She clearly explains the difference between the emotions felt in the heat of the moment and the feeling of fulfillment experienced when she recalls the deeds. Was she aware of the nobility of her actions? "I did not realize then," she says, "but the older I get, the more I feel I am very rich. I would not change anything. It's a wonderful feeling to know that today many people are alive and some of them married and have their children, and that their children will have children because I did have the courage and the strength."

Another story he gives is of one man on Jan 2, 2007.

"Wesley Autrey and his two daughters were waiting for the subway at the 137th St.-Broadway station in New York. All of a sudden, their attention was drawn to a young man having an epileptic fit. Wesley quickly intervened, using a pen to keep the man's jaw open. Once the fit was over, the young man got up but, still half-dazed, he stumbled and fell off the platform. While the sick man was lying on the tracks, Wesley saw the lights of an approaching train. He entrusted his daughters to a nearby woman to keep them away from the edge of the platform; then he jumped onto the tracks. He planned to carry the young man back to the platform but realized he wouldn't have time. So he threw himself over the man's body and pinned him on the ground in the drainage ditch between the two rails. Despite the conductor braking as hard as he could, the train passed almost completely over both of them. The

underside of the train left grease on Wesley's cap. Later on, Wesley told journalists: "I don't feel like I did something spectacular; I just saw someone who needed help. I did what I felt was right. I just said to myself, 'Somebody's got to help this guy or he's toast.' " xviii

Ricard concludes with this quote:

"According to Samuel and Pearl Oliner, emeritus professors at Humboldt University in California, who have devoted their careers to the sociology of altruism and more particularly to the study of the Just, the "Righteous Among the Nations," who saved many Jews during Nazi persecutions, altruism can be thought of as heroic when:

- *it has the aim of helping someone else;*
- *it involves a major risk or sacrifice;*
- *it is not linked to a reward;*
- *it is voluntary."* xix

Of course our own Christian heritage is full of examples of many people making both great and small sacrifices. My point here is to illustrate that love, whether you call it altruism, or selfless acts, or acting on the behalf of another's benefit, is still love.

The Apostle Paul puts it like this, *"Now there are three things that remain, faith, hope, and love. But the greatest of these is love."* Paul understood that ultimately love defined and was the final measure of everything.

> **LOVE DEFINES YOUR MOTIVES, YOUR VALUES, AND EVENTUALLY YOUR OUTCOMES. WITHOUT IT YOU GAIN NOTHING, YOU HAVE NOTHING, AND YOU ARE NOTHING.**

Questions to Consider:

How do you define love now?

What acts do you do to others that express love towards them?

Is that love recognized?

Are you doing it like Samuel and Pearl Oliner suggested? What acts do you do that fit this description?

- it has the aim of helping someone else;
- it involves a major risk or sacrifice;
- it is not linked to a reward;
- it is voluntary

List them here.

Can you name at least 3 ways in which love has benefited your life?

Love, the Fingerprint of the Divine

In this book we have given you a reference to understand Love from many points of view. Love is a cultural experience, a Christian mandate and proof of authenticity. In America, we are blessed to have a unique culture that was founded on the very ideas of love and an understanding that it comes from the divine. It is a right and also a responsibility at the same time. Once that connection with the divine is lost, so too is the responsibility lost. Once that connection has been completely eroded, then too the blessings it bestows upon us will disappear.

Love is also a personal experience. We have examined how love is both a personal responsibility to experience and to maintain. It is an attitude and presence of mind to choose to love. We get lost easily when we become overly self-indulgent and or self-seeking. We lose perspective when we serve ourselves only and neglect the service of others.

> In America, we are blessed to have a unique culture that was founded on the very ideas of love and an understanding that it comes from the divine.

We can also lose perspective when we ignore our own needs, desires, and calling. We can fail to connect with our own hearts and become disengaged from our own purpose in life. If we ignore our calling, the desires of our own heart, the inner convictions of our spirit, we can find ourselves discontent, frustrated, and depressed. We will find at that point that we are blaming others for how we feel.

Being true to yourself is a critical aspect of authentic love. It is impossible to encourage others to succeed if you are in a dungeon of self-defeat feeling controlled by everyone and everything.

Jesus was always true to himself, yet led by invitation. He looked out for the good of others while finding his purpose and identity within his relationship with the Father. He never wavered from his calling, yet always sought to build up others.

I will tell you where this became crystal clear and apparent like never before for myself. While working with so many in the intensive care inpatient mental hospital week after week I saw folks that had disengaged from ownership of their own lives. They simply stopped being responsible for expressing what they needed, desired, or were supposed to be about in their lives.

They were drowning in a sea of blame. They viewed themselves as being loving and kind. At the same time, they viewed others as being neglectful and unloving to them. This included husbands, wives, children, mothers, fathers, siblings, bosses, and many others. At some point they stopped seeing themselves as responsible for giving and receiving love in those relationships.

> **We cannot make someone love us. We can invite them into a loving relationship of mutual respect and affection.**

As we discussed in this book, what was wrong with the picture is their perspective of the personal responsibility of love. It is a process that we must take on. Once people could see where they disengaged, they could quickly see where they needed to pick it back up.

We have seen in this book that we cannot make someone love us. We can invite them into a loving relationship of mutual respect and affection. Since we cannot control others, we realize that we can control how we respond to others that are not loving, that control, manipulate, use, and dominate.

You control how you respond. It is a reasonable and even Godly trait to expect to be treated with respect and love, especially from those that have committed themselves to that relationship; mates, family, friends, church, and even society.

What I found that was so amazing when working with so many, was that no matter how messed up their situation was, people were always able to define what I call divine love within their own hearts.

This was true for Christians as well as atheists or non-believers. It did not seem to matter if folks were dealing with depression, suicidal thoughts, traumatic situations, or even psychosis like hearing several voices. They were all able to identify that they desired authentic love relationships and that in the end, this was more important than money, security, achievement, social status, or anything else you might want to list. The highest need of 99.9% of all my patients and clients was that of being able to give and receive love.

To me that was the single greatest revelation that I received from working with over 10,000 people over the past 10 years. Less that 10 would identify anything differently.

People can identify love. We know what it is even if we have never been shown it from our family of origin. That is one reason it hurts so very much when others that should love us, show the opposite.

This ability to identify love whatever the circumstances, is the very evidence of the fingerprint of the divine within every living soul. This is why when you hear the truth, you are responsible for how you respond to it. If you did not have that innate and ingrained understanding, then you could not be responsible for your knowledge or understanding.

But you are responsible. Even more than that, you are capable of embracing truth and enlightenment and changing any darkness within you into light and love.

Love is the deepest desire of your soul. It is a desire to connect with life and others as you knit your life together in this world. Love is inspired by and empowered by God Himself.

> Since love came from God, God has the right to define love. Love is definable, knowable, achievable and within your grasp. It starts in the heart and it's a choice.

1 John 4:9-19 "By this the love of God was manifested in us, that God has sent His only begotten Son into the world so that we might live through Him. In this is love, not that we loved God, but that He loved us and sent His Son to be the propitiation for our sins. Beloved, if God so loved us, we also ought to love one another. No one has seen God at any time; if we love one another, God abides in us, and His love is perfected in us. By this we know that we abide in Him and He in us, because He has given us of His Spirit. We have seen and testify that the Father has sent the Son to be the Savior of the world."

"Whoever confesses that Jesus is the Son of God, God abides in him, and he in God. We have come to know and have believed the love which God has for us. God is love, and the one who abides in love abides in God, and God abides in him. By this, love is perfected with us, so that we may have confidence in the day of judgment; because as He is, so also are we in this world. There is no fear in love; but perfect love casts out fear, because fear involves punishment, and the one who fears is not perfected in love. We love, because He first loved us."

Job 34:19 speaking of the Almighty God, *"who shows no partiality to princes and does not favor the rich over the poor, for they are all the work of his hands?"*

Questions which remain for us in the now.

Rate your life, on a scale of 1 to 10

How loving are you to your family of origin?

    Brothers, sisters, parents, relatives?

How loving are you to your current family?

    Mate and children?

How loving are you to your friends?

xx

How loving are you to your church?

How loving are you to your community?

How much do you invite others into a relationship with you?

In what ways do you invite others into a relationship with God?

How does your belief about yourself interfere with connecting with others, and connecting others to God?

Name 5 things you will do with the information learned in this book.

REFERENCES:

i "St. Thomas Aquinas, STh I-II, 26, 4, corp. art" . Newadvent.org. Retrieved 10-06-2015.

ii Goddard, Dwight; Henri Borel; James Legge; E.T.C. Werner; Frederic Balfour; Lao Tzu; Laozi; Paul Carus; Tse, Lao (2011-05-26). TAO TE CHING TAOISM ULTIMATE COLLECTION - 5 Expert Translations PLUS EXPLANATIONS for BEGINNERS and EVERYONE - For YOU to get EASY UNDERSTANDING of the Tao (also named Dao De Jing, Teh King, New Way) (Kindle Locations 2881-2882). Everlasting Flames Publishing. Kindle Edition.

iii https://en.wikipedia.org/wiki/The_Lady_in_Number_6

http://www.bing.com/videos/search?q=the+lady+in+%236+music+saved+my+life&FORM=VIRE3#view=detail&mid=5DACA3B54D973DFE12F45DACA3B54D973DFE12F4

ivhttp://www.mendeley.com/catalog/marital-status-happiness-17-nation-study/ taken 5/27/2013

vhttp://www.focusonthefamily.com/about_us/focusfindings/marriage/health-benefits-of-marriage.aspx taken 5/27/2013

vi Dambrun, Michae, Ricard, Matthieu Self-Centeredness and Selflessness: A Theory of Self-Based Psychological Functioning and Its Consequences for Happiness;

http://www.researchgate.net/publication/232521833

vii Michael J. Poulin is with the Department of Psychology, University at Buffalo, Buffalo, NY. Stephanie L. Brown and Dylan M. Smith are with the Department of Preventive Medicine, Stony Brook University, Stony Brook, NY. Amanda J. Dillard is with the Department of Psychology, Grand Valley State University, Allendale, MI.

'Giving to Others and the Association Between Stress and Mortality', Read More:

http://ajph.aphapublications.org/doi/abs/10.2105/AJPH.2012.300876?rfr_dat=cr_pub%3Dpubmed&rfr_id=ori%3Arid%3Acrossref.org&url_ver=Z39.88-2003

viii McGonigal Kelly: "How to make stress your friend" TED Talks, http://www.bing.com/videos/search?q=ted+talks+stress+relief&FORM=VIRE3#view=detail&mid=F54D455CF0DE444E1ADBF54D455CF0DE444E1ADB 10/20/2015

ix https://en.wikipedia.org/wiki/Christopher_Reeve

x http://transparentforchrist.com/

xi CLEMENS GAEBELEIN, ARNO, The Holy Spirit in the New Testament: An Exegetical Examination of Every New Testament Reference to the Spirit of God, Publication office "our Hope" 456 Fourth Avenue New York City http://www.biblebelievers.net/BibleStudies/kjcholyspirit.htm#TOC

xii Madden, Dennis "The God Partnership: A Spiritual Awakening Copyright 2015, God in Real Time LLC, Argyle, TX , (pgs 11,12, 89)

xiii Oberlin, Loriann Hoff (2005), Overcoming Passive-Aggression: How to Stop Hidden Anger From Spoiling Your Relationships, Career and Happiness , Perseus, p. 45

xiv American Psychiatric Association (2000). Diagnostic and Statistical Manual of Mental Disorders-IV. Washington, D.C.: American Psychiatric Association. pp. 733–734. ISBN 0890420629

xv Dambrun, and Ricard

xvi Ricard, Matthieu (2015-06-02). Altruism: The Power of Compassion to Change Yourself and the World (p. 76). Little, Brown and Company. Kindle Edition.

xvii Shantideva, The Way of the Bodhisattva: A Translation of the Bodhicharyavatara, trans. the Padmakara Translation Group, Shambhala Publications, 1997, p. 129.

xviii Ricard, Matthieu (2015-06-02). Altruism: The Power of Compassion to Change Yourself and the World (pp. 32-33,76, 136, 140-141, 849). Little, Brown and Company. Kindle Edition.

xix Oliner, Samuel and Pearl, *Do Unto Others: Extraordinary Acts of Ordinary People*, Basic Books, 2003, p. 21.

Other supportive references: Cohabitation Substantially Weakens the Marriage Relationship

Linda J. White and Maggie Gallagher. *The Case for Marriage: Why Married People Are Happier, Healthier, and Better Off Financially* (New York: Doubleday, 2000), 64.

Chris M. Wilson and Andrew J. Oswald, "How Does Marriage Affect Physical and Psychological Health? A Survey of the Longitudinal Evidence," Institute for Study of Labor Study Paper 1619 (Bon, Germany: Institute for the Story of Labor, May 2005), 16.

Robert M. Kaplan and Richard G. Kronick, "Marital Status and Longevity in the United States Population," *Journal of Epidemiology and Community Health* 60 (2006): 763.

Jonathan Gardner and Andrew Oswald, "How Is Mortality Affected by Money, Marriage and Stress?" *Journal of Health Economics* 23 (2004): 1181-1207.

Janice K. Kiecolt-Glaser and Tamara L. Newton, "Marriage and Health: His and Hers," *Psychological Bulletin* 127 (2001): 472-503.

Hyoun K. Kim and Patrick C. McKenry, "The Relationship Between Marriage and Psychological Well-Being: A Longitudinal Analysis," *Journal of Family Issues* 23 (2002), 905.

Glenn T. Stanton, *The Ring Makes All The Difference: The Hidden Consequences of Cohabitation and the Strong Benefits of Marriage* (Chicago: Moody Publishers 2011), 98-99.

ABOUT THE AUTHOR:

Dennis R. Madden, MA. LPC brings to the counseling forum both the Spiritual dynamics of an Ordained Minister and a Licensed Professional Counselor. He has a long history in Church Leadership, Pastoring, serving as youth pastor and other staff positions. Dennis is a public speaker, leading in seminars, weekend retreats, and church staff training. Dennis has always had a passion for evangelism and the gospel.

Dennis has a Professional Family Counseling Practice at 'Christian Counseling Associates' at the June Hunt Hope Center in Plano, TX.
Dennis has worked extensively in the Acute Care Mental Hospital setting, Minirth Faith Based inpatient psychiatric program and the Minirth Clinic.

While working with thousands of patients Dennis has developed the 'God in Real Time Christian Counseling Model' and has experienced phenomenal results. Dennis also has been working for a number of years in a cutting edge, clinical, outcome-based program in the health care industry, using motivational interviewing, positive psychological and solution focused approaches.

His Education includes: Bachelor's degree in Biblical studies from John Brown University; Two Masters Degrees from Southwestern Baptist Theological Seminary: One in Christian Education the other in Marriage and Family Therapy. Dennis also has had special studies under Dr. Jay Adams and Dr. Jay Vernon McGee. His other Biblical studies include courses taken with Quartz Hill School of Theology, Azusa Pacific University, Oklahoma Baptist University and others.

Dennis and his wife Linda have two grown daughters, and three granddaughters. They all reside in the Dallas/Fort Worth area where they enjoy regular family functions and the occasional getaway together.